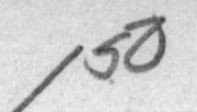

ARE YOU READY TO DIE?

Have you ever faced the fact of death—your own or someone else's? Or do you brush it off as a distasteful subject or a distant possibility? If you do indeed deny death, you are cheating yourself in every possible respect. For only in accepting and dealing with death honestly can you find the freedom to live.

This book shows you how to prepare for the end of your life, and how to cope with terminal illness and the death of those you love. BEFORE I WAKE draws upon the Bible, the ancients, artists, poets and philosophers as well as experts in medicine, psychology, religion, law and the funeral profession. It offers wise counsel and comfort, and fascinating, invaluable information on a subject that concerns us all.

Before I Wake

Paul R. Carlson

David C. Cook Publishing Co.
ELGIN, ILLINOIS—WESTON, ONTARIO

BEFORE I WAKE

First printing, February 1976
Second printing, August 1976

David C. Cook Publishing Co., Elgin, IL 60120
Printed in the United States of America
Library of Congress Catalog Number: 75-4042
ISBN: 0-912692-64-2

ACKNOWLEDGMENTS

Special acknowledgment is made to the following for permission to reprint copyrighted material:

American Medical Association: the "Uniform Donor Card."
Commission on Stewardship, National Council of Churches: from *Stewardship,* © 1974.
Forward Movement Publications: from *The Christian Facing Death,* by Carroll E. Simcox.
Harper & Row, Publishers, Inc.: from *A Doctor's Casebook in the Light of the Bible,* by Paul Tournier.
Los Angeles Times Syndicate: from "The Right to Live On," by Max Lerner. Reprinted by author's permission.
Macmillan Publishing Co.: from *On Death and Dying,* by Elisabeth Kubler-Ross. Copyright © 1969 by Elisabeth Kubler-Ross. Also from *Mere Christianity,* by C. S. Lewis. Copyright © 1943, 1945, 1952 by Macmillan Publishing Co., Inc.
National Funeral Directors Association: from *A Statistical Abstract of Funeral Service Facts and Figures of the United States, 1974 Edition,* by Vanderlyn R. Pine.
National Selected Morticians: from "Code of Good Funeral Practice."
The New York Times: from "The Living Will and the Will to Live," by David Dempsey. June 23, 1974. Copyright © 1974 by the New York Times Company.
World Vision International: from *God's Will and My Will.*

CONTENTS

1 In the Shadow of Death 15
2 Death with Dignity? 39
3 Where There's a Will 59
4 The Choice Is Yours 77
5 The Cost of the Alabaster Box 101
6 Not As a Stranger 119

PREFACE

Frank E. Farrell, the editor of *World Vision* magazine, recently wrote a column in which he described the Great Plague of 1665, which claimed the lives of some 70,000 Londoners.

During the terror-filled years, says Farrell, faithful ministers preached to terror-stricken crowds who, in the words of Horatius Bonar, "hung with breathless eagerness upon their lips, to drink in salvation ere the dreaded pestilence had swept them away to the tomb." Bonar, in *Words to Winners of Souls,* observes that God-fearing pastors during that period "preached as dying men to dying men."

Since then medical science has performed miracles. Some diseases have been eradicated, organs are now successfully transplanted, and scientists talk of the day when man might even be able to achieve physical immortality.

However, behind all of man's optimism about his longevity lurks the threat of war, famine, and the daily reminder that "it is appointed unto men once to die, but after this the judgment" (Heb. 9:27).

We may deny death, become enraged by its universal application, and bargain for release from its consequences, but in the solitude of our souls we know that man is born to die. Therefore, this book is intended to help the reader make crucial decisions before death strikes.

I have attempted to explore the options to the Christian view of death, from ancient paganism to that contemporary form which merely replaces the sacred cow with a sacred science.

Having conducted funeral services for hundreds, I have been singularly impressed by that infinite, qualitative difference between the funerals of believers and those of little or no faith. Karl Marx may have defined religion as an opiate, but I have seen too many families crushed by the reality of death in the absence of the "sure and certain hope in the resurrection through Jesus Christ our Lord."

Moreover, the Christian view of death provides far more than that proverbial pie in the sky in the sweet bye and bye. Rather, it gives meaning and purpose to life, the courage to face all that the fickle years have to offer, and yet boldly proclaim: "Nothing—not even death itself—shall separate us from the love of God in Christ Jesus." This has been the shared conviction of saints out of all traditions, races, and tongues down through the ages. No one can save, keep, and satisfy as does Jesus Christ in the hour of death.

Therefore, the first requirement for all men is to accept Christ as Savior and Lord before death. In that way, we will meet Him not as a stranger but as a Friend.

At the same time, not even the staunchest saint will escape some misgivings about his death or the death of a loved one. Jesus wept in the face of death, and so should we. For death means loss, separation, the relinquishing of those things which are precious in this life. This book is meant to help us deal with those emotions common to us all, knowing at the same time that "underneath are the everlasting arms."

Meanwhile, in addition to the host of destructive emotions that death raises within us, there are other nagging problems in our secular contemporary setting. For example, what are the rights of the dying and the bereaved in the face of modern medical science's search to prolong life? I can offer no panaceas, no answers, but provide a brief survey of current thinking in the field of bio-medical ethics and alternatives to dying in an impersonal and antiseptic setting.

There is a crucial need to get one's house in order before death. We all know that we should make a will and plan our estates. But we foolishly believe this can be put off until some elusive tomorrow. Unfortunately, tomorrow may be too late.

I have attempted to right the wrongs perpetrated against what has been called "the most maligned and misunderstood profession" in America today. What concerns me as a pastor is that every unfair attack on the funeral profession is an attack upon a family facing grief and bereavement. How can anyone place his confidence in a profession described as "the dismal trade"?

I am convinced that many attacks on the funeral profession represent a further erosion of confidence in those very institutions which have brought about the clear teaching of the Gospel and stability in national life and purpose. I believe that it is pagan to determine whether a funeral is good or bad merely on the basis of expense. To do so is to make cost accounting the measurement for a social, religious and personal process.

There may be unscrupulous funeral directors—just as there are unscrupulous clergymen, lawyers, and doctors—but, in 15 years as an extremely involved pastor, I have found the overwhelming number of them to be men of the highest integrity and of deep personal commitment. In fact, this book would have never been written had it not been for my association with an outstanding group of Christian men and women who arrange about 1,000 funerals a year.

May God lead and bless you as you seek His will before death.

Richmond Hill, New York PAUL R. CARLSON

BEFORE I WAKE

1. In the Shadow of Death

BERTHA WAS IN HER MID-FORTIES when she noticed a suspicious lump in her right breast. Her doctor was not optimistic when he examined her, and he said a radical mastectomy should be performed at once. Afterward he waited until Bertha was well on her way to recovery to tell her of the pathology report.

"The outlook isn't too good," he said as gently as possible. "The condition has spread, and I'm afraid we can't promise you more than two years to live." Bertha and her family tried their best to adjust to the clinical reality. However, after the two-year period, they were still "waiting for the inevitable."

In fact, Bertha was still alive six years later when her husband suddenly became ill and died. In her grief, she became aware that her two sons were increasingly becoming less sympathetic to her periods of pain and depression. The boys could no longer cope with a mother who continued chemotherapy and periodically entered the hospital when physical pain became unbearable.

Thirteen years after her surgery, Bertha's condition had so deteriorated that she could no longer care for herself. However, further complications developed. The unmarried son was unable to provide adequate care for her, while the other son, a father himself, refused to do so because, as he said, "I don't want my children to live with death."

So Bertha spent her last two years with a sister and her asthmatic husband. Her sister tried to make things as comfortable as possible for Bertha, even suggesting sometimes that she have someone come in to set her hair. "Why?" Bertha would ask. "You know it's just a matter of time."

But the hairdresser came, and afterward Bertha always felt better. Sometimes, it would boost her spirits enough so that she would temporarily take a renewed interest in a novel or TV soap opera.

Finally Bertha died—nine years after her husband, thirteen years beyond the doctor's limit, and fifteen years after the initial diagnosis and surgery. Her married son made the funeral arrangements in a distant city. However, his children were not allowed to attend their grandmother's funeral.

The whole family panicked on the night of the funeral service when the sister's husband suffered an acute asthmatic attack. Fortunately, the medicine he always carried helped him, and the services were held as planned. However, when physicians later suggested that living in Arizona might relieve his symptoms, Bertha's sister argued, "We have our roots here."

At the same time, the sister continued to nurse mixed feelings about the care she had given Bertha. Before Bertha's death, the sister could not talk about her without tears welling up in her eyes. Immediately afterward, however, she told friends: "This is the first time in two years that I don't have to apologize for an unmade bed in the living room."

If she experienced any hostility, it was toward the physician who had informed Bertha of her survival chances. "She could have enjoyed her final days," the sister said, "if only that doctor had not finished her life for her."

In a sense, Bertha's own testimony lent support to that view. Before her death, she often remarked: "I really died when the doctor told me that I would. With every new pain, I thought, 'This is it.' "

Apart from the psychodynamics of this particular case, the story raises a more general question: Should the dying patient know?

Psychiatrist Edward Gottheil replies that to tell some terminally ill persons of their fate may be as cruel as keeping a prisoner on death row before his execution. In a report to the American Psychiatric Association, he called for research to develop guidelines as to who can safely be told.

Dr. Gottheil questioned the current school of thought that it is more humane to be truthful with the fatally ill, "treating knowledge of impending death as a human right." Although some patients may accept such news calmly, he said, others sink into depression, react with anger, or simply blot the message from their minds. He reported that he and his associates found an increase in cases of mental depression paralleling the increasing practice of informing dying patients of their impending death.

One such person may welcome the news as an opportunity to wind up earthly affairs, he said, but another too ill to go to visit a new grandchild may react by abandoning all hope. And hope, he stressed, is a strong ally in the patient's will to fight. "We have all observed patients," he noted, "who, notwithstanding their medical condition, have given up and died, or fought and lived."

Therefore, Dr. Gottheil recommended "guidelines and principles which could be judiciously applied to specific cases to promote less depression, more communication and increased survival time." He suggested these questions be studied:

What should patients be told?

Which patients should be told (using personality tests and other measurements)?

When should they be told?

How should they be told (with finality or holding out hope that new research might change the odds)?

Who should tell them?

These variables can be controlled or manipulated, he explained, and then evaluated against actual outcomes, including the degree of happiness or despair, or the length of survival.

A companion dilemma is whether family members or nurses should be informed of the patient's prognosis. "Is it easier," asked Dr. Gottheil, "for them to know and engage in deceit if the patient doesn't know, or easier if they don't know?"

It is sufficient here to observe that in Bertha's case an apparent lack of professional discretion resulted in unnecessary anguish. The matter of a Christian witness to the dying is discussed later.

Meanwhile silence surrounding death has recently begun to fade in the wake of the new discipline of thanatology: the study of death and dying. On United States campuses, students have engaged in such projects as visiting the local morgue, detailing their own funeral arrangements, and even trying out a casket for size. They also have listened to tape-recorded interviews with dying patients, studied the death attitudes of ancient Jews, Greeks and Romans, and read current literature by theologians, sociologists, and psychologists.

"This is the first death-free generation in the history of the world," says Professor Robert Fulton, a sociologist who heads the Center for Death Education and Research at the University of Minnesota. He means that for the first time the vast bulk of youngsters now reach their majority without having experienced a death in the family. In cases where this is not true, Dr. Fulton says, young people generally did not attend the funeral or were absent when a death occurred.

In fact, his own center recently studied the cases of 560 bereaved persons and found that usually no family members were present at the deathbed and that most survivors learned of the death by a telephone call from a nurse, secretary, or other stranger. Therefore, says Dr. Fulton, "the point of the new college courses is to bring a new perspective to death—to show that it is natural and to counter some of the euphemistic devices our society uses to hide death and dying."

Professor Robert Kastenbaum, a psychologist at the University of Massachusetts, believes that people can "use the hypothetical fact of their own death to more fully evaluate the life they have been living." Dr. Kastenbaum, who is also editor of *Omega: the Journal of Death and Dying,* says of death, "It's the limit, something that defines and finishes what has gone before. I have found that a clear consciousness of death has made my life more precious to me moment by moment."

However, he readily concedes a breach in many cases between a person's ability to intellectualize about death and a real change in his emotional reaction. "There is a big difference between talk and a raw encounter with a death situation," he says. "We should not think that ability to talk about it is going to change the way we deal with it."

To support his conclusion, he cites an experiment in which mature housewives were asked to interview a man who they were told was a hospital patient. Some were informed that he was merely sick, while others were told he was terminally ill with abdominal cancer.

Dr. Kastenbaum says the patient received a warm reaction from those who thought he was simply ill. But the others seemed to be repelled, avoiding eye contact, and shrinking away from him. What was particularly significant was that among those repelled were housewives who earlier had expressed open attitudes toward dying.

"Death is still a fearful, frightening happening," says Dr. Elisabeth Kubler-Ross, who has done extensive research in this field. "And the fear of death is a universal fear even if we think we have mastered it on many levels. What has changed is our way of coping and dealing with death and dying and our dying patients."

In her pioneer work, Dr. Kubler-Ross has isolated and identified five stages through which the terminally ill pass before death: (1) denial, (2) anger, (3) bargaining, (4) depression, and finally, (5) acceptance.

In her book, *On Death and Dying,* she explains that during the initial stage of denial most of the patients interviewed reacted thus to the prognosis: "No, not me. It cannot be true." To support their denial systems, some would go to extreme lengths to convince themselves that the X rays were mixed up, or that the pathological reports could not have been prepared so quickly. Others would vainly shop for other doctors, hoping the initial diagnosis was incorrect.

Although some form of denial is common to all terminally ill patients, Dr. Kubler-Ross says, the most anxious are those who have been informed brusquely or prematurely of their true condition.

"Denial functions as a buffer after unexpected shocking news," she explains. "It allows the patient to collect himself and, with time, mobilize other, less radical defenses." Later, she adds, the same patient may be willing—or even happy and relieved—to talk with someone else about his impending death. However, such dialogue can and must take place only under conditions set by the patient himself.

In cases in which death is not imminent, Dr. Kubler-Ross says, both the individual and his family often find it easier to discuss the issues and to prepare for the future security of the household. "To postpone such talks," she advises, "is often not in the service of the patient but serves our own defensiveness."

When denial can no longer be maintained, most patients find feelings of anger, rage, envy, and resentment welling up within themselves. The next logical question becomes: "Why me?"

"In contrast to the stage of denial," says Dr. Kubler-Ross, "this stage of anger is very difficult to cope with from the point of view of family and staff. The reason for this is the fact that this anger is displaced in all directions and projected onto the environment at times almost at random."

Occasionally anger and resentment will be manifested by comparing one's sense of self-worth with someone else. But often the hostility is directed against the doctors and nurses. If a visiting family is greeted without cheerfulness and anticipation, Dr. Kubler-Ross observes, loved ones will often "either respond with grief and tears, guilt or shame, or avoid future visits, which only increases the patient's discomfort and anger." Family members must try to understand the anger's source and that it probably is not directed at them personally.

Dr. Kubler-Ross counsels people to appreciate the fact that the terminally ill realize that all of their well-laid plans have been for nothing. Gone are such hopes as using some hard-earned money for a few years of rest and enjoyment, or for travel and pursuit of hobbies. "Maybe we too would be angry," she notes, "if all our life activities were interrupted so prematurely."

Generally there comes a point at which rage is replaced by bargaining. In effect, the patient reasons: "If God . . . did not respond to my angry pleas, He may be more favorable if I ask nicely."

"The bargaining is really an attempt to postpone," says Dr. Kubler-Ross. "It has to include a prize offered 'for good behavior,' it also sets a self-imposed 'deadline' . . . and it includes an implicit promise that the patient will not ask for more if this one postponement is granted."

In one case, she records, a woman on the brink of death got her wish to attend her oldest child's wedding. However, when she returned exhausted to the hospital, she immediately reminded the staff: "Now don't forget I have another son!"

"None of our patients have 'kept their promise,' " Dr. Kubler-Ross says understandingly. "The patient just described was unwilling to face us again unless we acknowledged the fact that she did have another son whose wedding she also wanted to witness."

Although writing from a scientific perspective, Dr. Kubler-Ross has been impressed by the number of bargains which have been made directly with God. Such promises are often expressed in terms of better church attendance or a recommitment to the Christian life. Since these bargains are often associated with guilt, she believes that a sensitive chaplain or physician can do much in an interdisciplinary setting to relieve irrational fears and an unconscious wish for punishment.

After this bargaining process, the terminally ill enter the fourth stage, depression, when their symptoms can no longer be denied. Dr. Kubler-Ross explains that depression takes two forms: reactive, and preparatory. In the first instance, the patient is concerned about such things as a loss of self-esteem caused by disfiguring surgery, the mounting financial burden associated with prolonged hospital care, or the inability to provide any longer for the needs of family members.

In dealing with reactive depression, Dr. Kubler-Ross says, a husband can be supportive to a wife who has just undergone breast surgery, maintaining her sense of femininity and self-esteem. Moreover, social workers and chaplains can be of help in the reorganization of a household, especially when youngsters or lonely old people are involved.

But other factors must be taken into consideration in dealing with preparatory depression, which is not associated with any past loss but rather with a reaction to impending losses.

"The patient is in the process of losing everything and everybody he loves," Dr. Kubler-Ross observes. "If he is allowed to express his sorrow, he will find a final acceptance much easier, and he will be grateful to those who can sit with him during this stage of depression without constantly telling him not to be sad."

Unlike the verbal interaction which takes place during the period of reactive depression, this second stage is often marked by the patient's silence. "There is no or little need for words," says Dr. Kubler-Ross. "It is much more a feeling that can be mutually expressed and is often done better with a touch of a hand, a stroking of the hair, or just a silent sitting together. This is the time when the patient may just ask for a prayer, when he begins to occupy himself with things ahead rather than behind," she continues. "It is a time when too much interference from visitors who try to cheer him up hinders his emotional preparation rather than enhances it."

Moreover, Dr. Kubler-Ross emphasizes that a patient must be able to work through his anguish and anxieties if he is to pass on to the fifth stage of acceptance and die in peace. In cases in which this occurs, the terminally ill will reach that point at which they will neither be angry nor depressed about their fate. However, Dr. Kubler-Ross stresses, "Acceptance should not be mistaken for a happy stage. It is almost void of feelings."

For those who are completely bedridden, she says, there will be an increasing need to extend the hours of sleep—not a sleep of hopeless resignation, but rather a sleep that prepares the individual for "the final rest before the long journey."

As the patient's circle of interest diminishes, Dr. Kubler-Ross adds, this is also the time when the family generally needs more support and understanding than a dying loved one. He has found some peace and acceptance, but the family must go on working out the grief process.

Since Dr. Kubler-Ross completed her landmark study, an Iowa newsman with terminal cancer has started a courageous movement for people who, like himself, have a severely limited life expectancy. To free himself of impatience, loneliness, and depression, Orville Kelly of Burlington, Iowa, founded MTC: Make Today Count. Chapters of the organization are now reportedly sprouting like dandelions and drawing interest from other terminally ill persons in France, Germany, and Spain.

After receiving his diagnosis, Kelly found it impossible to live with his fits of depression and decided that there must be a better way than self-pity and anger. "So I decided to deal openly and honestly with the facts," he says. "And I'm a happier man now for it." Kelly believes the key is to refrain from dwelling on the future. "Just get the most," he says, "out of each minute of each day."

Because Kelly must be hospitalized occasionally, the Reverend James Bracher, associate pastor of the Second Congregational Church, Greenwich, Connecticut, serves as MTC's managing director, a post he acquired after Kelly spoke in his church. "As Orville says," remarks Mr. Bracher, "we're all terminal in a way. The emphasis at MTC is whatever members in particular chapters want it to be. But underneath it all there is this powerful thought: they're not dying so much as they're learning to live. They are giving one another courage. Their lives are sermons for all."

Rather than engaging in an exchange of agonies, Mr. Bracher reports, MTC chapters sometimes foster discussions on wills and financial questions as well as on other matters of concern to the terminally ill. "The springboard," he notes, "is hope."

Pointing to a recent study by the American Medical Association, Mr. Bracher further observes that "the people who cope best with cancer have strong inner resources, a good self-image, and strong family support."*

Returning to Bertha's case, in the absence of hard data it is difficult to determine what her deepest feelings were during her ordeal. But all the evidence indicates that she and her family would have been aided immeasurably by Dr. Kubler-Ross' work and Orville Kelly's courage.

Moreover, Bertha's case raises pressing ques-

*Persons wishing to form MTC chapters may write to the Rev. James Bracher, Second Congregational Church, 139 East Putnam Avenue, Greenwich, CT 06830.

tions as to how family members themselves work through the grief process. To help their members understand the nature and necessity of grief, the session of the First Presbyterian Church, Jamaica, New York, has prepared an excellent pamphlet in which Christians are called upon to recognize that "the closer the relationship, the more acute this reaction will be." In addition, they correctly observe:

> Grief sometimes includes feelings of guilt. We may feel that we have not done all that we might have for those whom we love. When such a person dies, we become acutely aware of our failures in the relationship. Moreover, there is often considerable resentment at being deprived of one upon whom we have been dependent, and this heightens our feelings of guilt. Because the funeral is our last chance to demonstrate our love for the one who has died, we are tempted to make it as lavish as possible. Without realizing it, people often attempt to assuage their guilt and "make up" for their shortcomings by spending more than they can afford on the funeral.

When a sense of deep personal loss is coupled with the reality of heavy debt, the session notes, "feelings of resentment and guilt toward the deceased are often heightened rather than healed by this pattern of over-expenditure." Finally, they urge church members to realize that the grief-stricken are swept with various painful and confusing feelings. "If they try to suppress and ignore these normal reactions to death," these elders state, "the feelings remain like hidden poison, troubling them in years to come."

When psychologists speak of grief work, they mean that the bereaved must face and work out these painful and confusing feelings as the pathway to freedom from grief. Meanwhile, on occasion some mourners underreact or overreact to grief by either turning coldly impersonal and efficient, or completely falling to pieces. When such symptoms persist, the individual withdraws from life and demonstrates unprovoked suspicion or anger at others. Professional help may be needed to resolve his inner conflicts.

Also, laymen must recognize that physicians, funeral directors, and clergymen are not immune from normal human reactions to death. They may intellectualize more about it, but they share all of the common human strengths and weaknesses at the emotional level. In fact, Dr. Hans Mausch, of the University of Missouri Medical School, contends that the health-care professional must also pass through Dr. Kubler-Ross' five psychological stages of denial, anger, bargaining, depression, and acceptance.

Dr. Mausch, chief of the school's behavioral sciences section, says the physician's initial reaction is to deny the diagnosis because he doesn't want to admit his inability to cure the patient. Then his anger is aroused when he can no longer brush aside death's inevitability and his own powerlessness.

The bargaining stage is generally the most subtle, both for the patient and the professional, Dr. Mausch observes. There are choices available: hook up tubes and prescribe medication to stretch life a little longer, or ask forgiveness of God or yourself with the hope of delaying death a few months. During the depression period, Dr. Mausch advises doctors, nurses, and technicians to vent their own emotions. "Don't be afraid to cry," he counsels. "Don't lose control, but don't hold back the tears in the presence of a dying patient."

When professionals arrive at the acceptance stage, Dr. Mausch says, this reaction should not be confused with resignation or interpreted as abandoning all hope. In fact, Dr. Edward F. Dobihal, Jr., director of the department of religious ministries at Yale-New Haven Hospital in Connecticut, specifically advises doctors never to suggest that nothing more can be done for a person. After informing a family member of the prognosis, Dr. Dobihal says, the professional should then determine "what can be done to help the patient with living until he can live no more."

At the same time, Dr. Mausch has observed that, in addition to sharing the five psychological stages of death, health-care professionals also experience the four universals realized by the dying patient. The first, fear of abandonment, may be manifested for the professional in the loss of the patient or in the apparent loss of skills required to save him.

Second, the universal of hope is adjusted to conform with reality. This hope is not for the continuation of life, which is impossible, but for death without pain or for an attitude of understanding on the part of family, friends, and colleagues.

The third universal is concern over unfinished business. For the medical staff as well as the patient this may involve specific business such as the signing of contracts or making a reassuring statement or apologizing for a thoughtless action.

Finally, health-care specialists share in that last universal of the conspiracy of silence. "Health-care workers receive gratification through healing, through giving," says Dr. Dobihal. "When they can no longer give, there is no gratification, so the terminal patient is avoided. Discussion with him is restricted for fear the topic of death will arise."

This is as true for nurses as it is for physicians. A head nurse in the neurological intensive-care unit of a major New York City hospital recently appealed to clergymen to recognize that the entire medical team is composed of very human beings.

Although families of the critically ill sometimes think of doctors and nurses as impatient and gruff, this nurse remarked: "Because you feel so bad yourself, you try to distance yourself from the situation." Expressing her own feelings of loss and guilt, she told of becoming involved with a dying patient and her family. "But," she added, "I'll never get that involved again. You have to develop your own defense mechanisms . . . and learn to forgive yourself. I recognize now that sometimes I have to withdraw for my own mental health."

A dying student nurse lamented the fact that her training emphasized that it can be detrimental both to the patient and the medical team to meet pathology with pathology. That is, the professional must be aware of his own inner feelings and conflicts before he can be helpful in dealing with those of a patient, another human being.

Writing in the *American Journal of Nursing*, the student nurse conceded that all this was true. "But for me," she added, "fear is today and dying is now." She wrote to her colleagues: "You slip in and out of my room, give me medications, and check my blood pressure. Is it because I am a student nurse myself, or just a human being, that I sense your fright? And your fear enhances mine. Why are you afraid?" she asked. "I am the one who is dying. I know you feel insecure, don't know what to say, don't know what to do. But please believe me, if you care, you can't go wrong."

This poignant story points up the fact that doctors, nurses, funeral directors, and even clergymen, react to death differently when it strikes them as individuals or members of their families. Then all pretense of professionalism often is discarded.

An elderly pastor after 45 years in the ministry confessed to his own unsettled feelings while waiting to die. Recalling how he had often preached on Paul's personal testimony of life and death (I Cor. 15), he remarked, "Thanks, Paul, for those bracing words. But, dear Paul, I have news for you. From my little corner, the sting of death still stings!"

Even more revealing was a recent double tragedy

which left an eight-month-old girl an orphan. According to the police, the baby's 30-year-old mother, a nursing supervisor, suffered a heart attack while rushing to aid a patient in cardiac arrest. The mother died while the patient lived. Apparently unable to cope with his grief, the infant's father was found dead in his home two days later, a gun near his body. He was a funeral director.

Both laymen and professionals must, by the grace of God, exhibit more understanding for one another. Both also need to learn how to deal more effectively with their own anxieties. For, as Robert L. Scheig of the University of Connecticut Medical School suggests, the terminally ill can only be effectively treated after the members of the healing and helping professions themselves come to terms with their own mortality.

In light of all of these factors, one can engage in some educated guesses concerning the reactions of the players in the drama of Bertha's lingering illness and eventual death. If Dr. Mausch is correct, the family physician was no mere detached onlooker when he informed Bertha of her life expectancy. But we'll never know at what stage he was in the grief process. Did he himself feel pangs of abandonment based upon a fear of lost skills or the censure of his colleagues? Was he angry or depressed?

Other clinical studies indicate that Bertha's sons were not unusual in their behavior when they began to lose patience with their mother after their father's unexpected death. Sigmund Freud considered a father's death as "the most important event, the most poignant loss, of a man's life." But these boys had been giving all of their attention to a mother whose death was professionally diagnosed as almost imminent.

On the other hand, Avery Weisman, a professor at Harvard Medical School and a member of the Euthanasia Council's Medical Advisory Committee, cites the case of a father whose little boy had a remission after doctors had lost all hope for the child's survival. When death ultimately came, this man was unable to express grief, although he complained of symptoms similar to those which his son experienced when he first became ill. But the grief itself had been deeply felt when hope vanished before the temporary reprieve.

Although social convention required otherwise, in a sense the father actually responded negatively to the extension of his son's life. "When death and dying came a second time," says Dr. Weisman, "the man was closed off. Grief had come before. He could not repeat his sadness, and he felt guilty. His guilt prevented him from acknowledging the finality of his son's death."

This case is suggestive of the emotions experienced by Bertha's sons, because they too had been faced with a deadline which came and then passed long before their mother's death. However, we must remember that people respond differently to the death of a child and that of an adult.*

*For a deeply moving personal account of the loss of children, readers are referred to *The View from a Hearse* by Joseph Bayly (Elgin: David C. Cook Publishing Co., 1969, rev. 1973).

At the same time, the actions and reactions of Bertha's older son are significant for two other reasons. It is interesting that he felt obliged to handle the funeral arrangements himself. This fact might well indicate that he was determined to take on this burden to assuage his own guilt because he had refused his mother a final earthly home and had rejected the idea of his family living with death.

Moreover, most psychologists would reject the older son's determination to isolate his own youngsters from their dying grandmother. In fact, Dr. Kubler-Ross in her second book, *Questions and Answers on Death and Dying,* argues that the earlier a child is exposed to death in the family, the easier will be his acceptance without fear of his own death.

However, she voices a note of caution when a child appears to adjust well to death, especially the death of a parent. She tells of a calm little boy whose only idiosyncrasy was his insistence on placing an apple outside his window. When asked why, he replied: "Maybe Mommy [who loved apples] will come back and not be mad at me anymore."

Meanwhile, the reactions of Bertha's sister are interesting in that they reveal a common ambivalence toward the death of a loved one. She cried at the thought of her sister's condition, but, on the other hand, she expressed relief when her own household routine was no longer interrupted, a common feeling often laden with guilt.

In addition, she may have identified Bertha's sickness and death with her own mortality. This is indicated both by her tears and by her desire not to be abandoned by moving to Arizona, far away from friends and loved ones.

The asthmatic husband's acute attack on the evening of the funeral further suggests the emotional turmoil confronting both husband and wife. The funeral may well have sharpened the weakened husband's sense of the uncertainty and precariousness of life, while his wife possibly reinforced her resolve to stay close to home, should her asthmatic mate abandon her in death. However, there is also that tragic picture of Bertha herself waiting for the inevitable, even objecting to having her hair set, fearful that death could strike with each new pain.

Although Bertha's relationship to Christ and His Church is not known, this is where the role of the Gospel, reflected in the work of a sensitive pastor or hospital chaplain, could have come into play.

First, active identification with the Church's teaching ministry could have been extremely supportive during those years of pain and uncertainty. For, as Dr. Herbert Anderson, assistant professor of practical theology at Princeton Theological Seminary, has observed, the Church raises certain theological issues regarding death and dying:

> There is first an understanding that life involves both its quantitative and qualitative aspects. On the one hand, the Christian recognizes that "the Lord giveth, and the Lord taketh away"; but, on the other, he affirms that real living does not merely consist of the

"abundance of the things which he possesseth."

There is the further understanding that death cannot be viewed in the abstract as a friend, blessing, or mystery. The Christian tradition rather equates death with sin—and identifies it as an enemy to be ultimately destroyed.

There is beyond that recognition the firm conviction that life exists beyond the grave, a conviction that helps to reduce fear in the mind and heart of the believer.

Moreover, beyond the belief that the Christian himself will survive death, there is that central truth of Christ's own victory over the grace—that His Resurrection symbolizes the absolute vindication of God.

Finally, the Church teaches that God has "a great surprise" in store for those who love Him. And that "great surprise" is in our best interest.

Dr. Anderson has added Christian thoughts to Dr. Kubler-Ross' secular model for the management of death. "Courage is the flip side of despair," he says. "And gratitude is the flip side of bargaining." Moreover, he says, "Hope is the flip side of isolation. As Christians, we hope *with* rather than hope *for,* because isolation is the enemy of hope."

However, beyond his teaching function, the pastor is a *minister*. He can counsel those who face the tragedy and glory of death, not as one who knows all the answers, but rather as one who genuinely cares. Also, he can listen when doctors and nurses—or even family members—are unable to share in that language of loving silence.

Above all, the sensitive pastor or hospital chaplain can witness to believer and unbeliever alike that "every burden, every bereavement, every sorrow, has been foreseen and fore-appointed by a Wisdom that cannot err and by a Love that cannot change."

That every cloud that spreads above
And veileth love, itself is love.

In that faith we walk, even through the valley of the shadow of death, fearing no evil, knowing that God is with His own.

2. Death with Dignity?

AUSTRALIAN NOBEL PRIZE WINNER Sir Macfarlane Burnet has made it clear that he has no desire to die more than once. Now in his 70s, he insists that such a possibility now exists because modern medical science has become too successful in its ability to prolong life. And he should know, for he won his Nobel Prize in medicine in 1960 for work that made possible transplantation of human organs. Consequently, he carries this card with him:

> I request that, in view of my age, any prolonged unconsciousness, whether due to accident, heart attack or strokes, should be allowed to take its course without benefit of an intensive-care or resuscitation ward.

Sir Macfarlane's rationale is clear: "Death in the

old should be accepted as something always inevitable and sometimes positively desirable. Doctors should not compel old people to die more than once."

Unfortunately, however, his personal position can pose a host of problems for his attending physicians and family members. The medical profession's rigorous training is geared to extend and preserve human life. What's more, many doctors are often loathe to "pull the plug" because of moral convictions and/or the fear of malpractice suits which recently have risen steadily.

Moreover, physicians are constantly besieged by relatives to use every means possible to extend the life of a loved one, even when it only means the extension of agony for all concerned. Even when irreversible brain damage has occurred, hope lies eternal in the human breast. There is often that lingering notion that a miracle drug or cure will somehow spare the life of a beloved parent, spouse, or child.

Such problems are only compounded when a doctor believes that he must bear every victory or defeat. Only a mature physician can look death squarely in the eye and say: "The Lord gave, and the Lord hath taken away; blessed be the name of the Lord" (Job 1:21). This may appear callous and lacking in proper bedside manner, but there are limits beyond which modern medical science cannot go.

A devoutly Christian doctor recently informed a woman that he had done all that was humanly possible to preserve the life of her husband of half a century. He said tenderly, "I can keep on using artificial means, or I can let nature take its course. What should I do?"

A warm relationship of trust had developed between the family and the physician over the years. So, the woman indicated that the latter course was probably wiser. As her husband quietly entered his eternal rest a short time later, she was buoyed by a lifelong Christian conviction: "We are confident, I say, and willing rather to be absent from the body, and to be present with the Lord" (II Cor. 5:8).

However, the strongest saint cannot watch a loved one die without deep feelings of ambivalence. He, as others, will be torn by the pain of loss, separation, and even abandonment. Moreover, when he has faced the trauma of discarding artificial means for preserving life, there is always the possibility that guilt will ask, "Did I make the right decision? Could more have been done?"

Of course, the Christian intellectually accepts the fact that death is part of life. What's more, theologians concur that God does not require extraordinary means to be employed when ordinary means are unable to sustain life. But such concessions merely raise other questions.

There is the problem of defining death itself in view of recent advances in medical science. It is no longer possible to equate death with the cessation of the heartbeat. This was graphically illustrated when a group of men went on trial for fatally beating a man whose heart was later used for a surgical transplant. In their defense, the suspects pleaded that the victim was not dead when the transplant took place. If anyone was guilty of homicide, they contended, it was the surgical team. To complicate matters, physicians differed among themselves as to the time, locus, and cause of death. One doctor pronounced the victim dead when his brain and respiratory functions ceased; another disagreed.

Because of such conflicts, a committee of scientists, physicians, lawyers, and theologians met at Harvard to formulate these criteria for brain death:

1. The patient is unreceptive and unresponsive.
2. The patient shows no signs of movement or breathing.
3. The patient has no reflexes.
4. The patient's electroencephalogram is flat.

Some would argue that the electroencephalogram merely confirms the other criteria, which are considered conclusive if repeated after a 24-hour period. Excluded from such tests are persons with an internal temperature below 90 degrees and those ingesting depressants for the central nervous system.

In spite of such safeguards, critics charge that these criteria are meant to promote the social benefit of organ transplants. And advocates are doing little to discourage such interpretations of this new definition of "brain death."

"There is indeed a life-saving potential in the new definition," says Dr. Henry Beecher. "For when accepted, it will lead to greater availability than formerly of essential organs in viable condition for transplantation. Can society afford to discard the organs of such patients if they can be used to restore health to salvageable patients?"

However, Dr. Robert M. Veatch, an expert in biomedical ethics, is among those who fear that this line of reasoning elevates "the good of the collective society over against that of an individual." He says, "Whenever we get to the position of arguing that a new definition of death should be adopted because it would provide organs, we have made an unconscionable violation of an individual's right to life. On the other hand, if all we are saying is that we should look at what we have always meant by the concept of death and make it more precise because, as a by-product, we are able to serve a social function, then I find no fault with that position."

Lurking in the background is the explosive issue of euthanasia, or mercy killing. Here again both the professional community and the general public are sharply divided. The very term "euthanasia" conjures up memories of Bavarian scientists who as early as 1931 were publicly discussing sterilization and mercy killing for mental patients. It was just a short step to its implementation when the Nazis decreed that both Jews and Gypsies no longer possessed the right to life.

American juries have been generally sympathetic to those who have felt compelled to release someone from the final agony of death. A Long Island jury recently decided whether a physician actively abetted the death of a tragically ill patient, or whether the man died of mounting multiple illnesses, any one of which could have killed him. When the jury handed down a not-guilty verdict, the courtroom crowd cheered, wept, and embraced one another. Columnist Max Lerner wrote:

> The people themselves—the jury and spectators who were neither lawyers nor experts but simply humans—cut through all the technical stuff, straight to the heart of the human and moral issue. They expressed a mounting conviction among many people, perhaps most, that society goes to absurd lengths to keep patients alive who are, in effect, vegetables, anguished in their suffering, dead in every way but the final stopping of heart and brain.
>
> We deceive ourselves if we think these are decisions only for doctors, lawyers, legislators and churchmen. There isn't one of us who may not have to face, in his own life or some other's, the ravaging diseases which make life hopeless and intolerable. What choice, in moral and human terms, is the right one?

Unfortunately, an individual confronted with this question will discover no easy answers. Rather, he will have to wrestle with the existing realities in light of his own moral and religious convictions. Lerner himself believes that the first principle involved is the absolute priority of the patient's will to live: "Perhaps I deceive myself, but I think I shall want to stick around until the last possible gasp, pain or no pain, hope or no hope, as long as consciousness is there. But if the patient's will to live is replaced by a will to have his life end, the answer must lie in some consensus of doctors and family and others who care about him and his life."

What Lerner would avoid is bequeathing upon the medical profession the right to determine which patients shall live. That awesome power, he suggests, would turn doctors into gods who are also zombies.

A U.S. Senate special committee on aging recently began an inquiry into issues related to death with dignity. From the outset of the hearings, witnesses sharply disagreed on fundamental questions. While a physician held that all efforts should be taken to preserve life, a psychiatrist responded that certain practices should be abandoned because they turn the dying patient into a medical pincushion. Then he indicated he was opposed to all efforts to codify right to die legislation into law.

Some personal notes were injected into the debate. A 94-year-old retired college president wept as he told of how nurses forced open the jaws of his dying wife to make her eat. The committee chairman, Senator Frank Church (Democrat-Idaho), recalled that doctors had only given him six months to live when cancer was discovered—back in 1947!

These lawmakers also heard of attempts to press state legislatures to enact bills allowing a person to sign a legal document requesting permission to die under certain circumstances. Contending that 75 percent of America's physicians already practice death with dignity, one proponent argued that such a measure would tend to relieve the doctor of possible liability in cases where active treatment is stopped. Such legislation would permit a close relative to decide when the patient is mentally incompetent.

When such patients have neither a guardian nor close relatives, the decision would be left to three staff members of any recognized hospital. This proposal was strongly contested by Senator Charles Percy (Republican-Illinois), who hinted of avarice replacing compassion when survivors might expect monetary gain. "Human nature being what it is," he said, "you can always find unscrupulous physicians, clergy and family willing to shut off medical care to people in intensive care."

Moreover, while thousands reportedly already have signed the living will to be spared a prolonged and agonizing death, so-called right-to-die legislation raises many perplexing questions. Lord Brock, a British physician, argues that the medical profession bears a special ethical duty to avoid euthanasia in either its positive or negative forms.

"As an ordinary citizen I must expect that the killing of an unwanted can be legalized by an Act of Parliament," he says. "But as a doctor I must know that there are certain things which are part of the ethics of our profession that an Act of Parliament cannot justify or make acceptable. . . . We may accept the need for euthanasia on social grounds, but we cannot accept that doctors should implement it."

David Dempsey, in an article in the *New York Times,* delineates the argument of the right-to-die critics:

> The real danger, these opponents point out, lies in an overly simplistic attitude toward dying in general, primarily the view that a "good" death is something that can be anticipated and managed. What may appear to be an individual right, moreover, is actually entwined in a number of social relationships. Before a verdict can be rendered, they say, at least four crucial aspects of the problem need to be examined:
>
> 1) Does a person, in fact, have a constitutional right to die? If so, is the right always in his best interest?
> 2) Does death by choice represent medicine's best answer to the admittedly difficult question of incurable and/or terminal illness?
> 3) Does society have an investment in human life—and the concept of its sacredness—that overrides the individual, if not legally, at least morally? (Conversely, does the notion of "easy death" give society a dangerous weapon to regulate population in a world burdened with too many unproductive people?)
> 4) Does the right to die, in effect, sanction

> unconscious, self-destructive impulses in people? Is it another escapist symptom in a world looking for easy answers to the human dilemma?

Ironically, Princeton theologian Paul Ramsey was one of the first scholars to speak out against excessive medical measures for the terminally ill. But he now argues that the notion of death with dignity has taken on certain elements of the soap opera. To suggest that death is an occurrence as natural as birth is, for Ramsey, "whistling before the darkness descends." Far from there ever being any dignity in death, he says, death is the ultimate indignity.

As a Methodist, he clings to the traditional Christian view that death entered into the world as "the wages of sin," the divine punishment for Adam's fall. Ever since, he says, Christians have regarded death as the enemy. To be sure, Ramsey argues, the sacrificial death of Jesus Christ has redeemed man for eternal life. But even that sacrifice did nothing to prevent death from being a shattering separation of soul and body.

Ethicist Ramsey introduces a historical observation into the right-to-die debate. Were it not for Christianity's proper dread of death, he says, it would not have laid the foundations of Western medicine by demonstrating compassionate concern for the sick. It is foolish to invest death with a bogus dignity because it may, in fact, hinder care for the dying by establishing a new set of illusions. Therefore, he contends, a true humanism still depends on a dread of death.

Apart from these ethical, legal, and theological considerations, individuals react quite differently to this still universal dread of death. Moreover, their reactions are motivated by a wide range of medical, emotional, and pragmatic considerations.

A distraught father recently wrote a national clergy periodical concerning self-destructive tendencies alluded to by right-to-die opponents. In this unusual case, the Gospel itself played an unwitting role in the death of the man's emotionally disturbed son. The boy had attended a funeral service at which the minister said the deceased had entered a new life free of pain and torment. A short time later the boy decided that the only way he could share this eternal bliss was to kill himself. He promptly did so.

Of course this case borders on the bizarre. But it serves as a warning that unconscious drives may be operating in certain people which can lead to their self-destruction. If the hope of the redeemed could trigger this kind of response in an emotionally disturbed boy, then it is also possible that right-to-die legislation could put the state's blessing on suicidal tendencies in some people.

However, there are more common responses. One has been cited by Dr. Avery Weisman, a professor at Harvard Medical School and a member of the Euthanasia Council's Medical Advisory Committee. In spite of his affiliation with the council, Dr. Weisman has never signed a so-called living will.

His reasoning, based upon a long career, is amazingly blunt: "I don't want someone pulling the plug on me because they need the bed. I know some doctors that I wouldn't want in charge of telling me the time of day, let alone the time to die."

Meanwhile, the case of Mrs. Arthur E. Morgan, wife of the former head of the Tennessee Valley Authority, demonstrates that time and circumstance can alter the opinions of even the strongest right-to-die advocates. Earlier Mrs. Morgan had argued in a widely circulated letter that "one should be allowed to drink the hemlock in some dignified and simple way." However, although she later became blind, deaf, and senile, she and her family opted against the hemlock, and she died instead in a nursing home at the age of 94.

Obviously medical science is making tremendous leaps against diseases once considered incurable. A nurse in her thirties decided to go ahead and marry even though she was given only 18 months to live after cancer had spread to her lungs.

Here medical science conspired against its own death warrant because of cancer research advancements. This patient's life was extended when scientists at the Ohio State University Medical School discovered that immunity could be built up through regular injections of a booster compound called transfer factor. This factor is derived from the blood of persons who have been in close contact with the patient and either have had cancer and recovered or never developed cancer at all.

The medical profession would be the first to

admit that it is not the final arbiter in matters of life and death. On the human level, the age, the disease, and the patient's own wishes are powerful factors to be considered. And behind the tubes and technology stands a God who has numbered all our days.

Those who have lived a rich and full life generally come to accept *experientially* that:

> The days of our years are threescore years and ten; and if by reason of strength they be fourscore years, yet is their strength labour and sorrow; for it is soon cut off, and we fly away (Ps. 90:10).

Our common human mortality was not lost to a 70-year old woman who wrote to a popular columnist shortly after learning she was a terminal case:

> As I lay here in the hospital after learning the bitter truth, I wept for three hours, not because I am going to die, but because of what medical science can do to keep me alive. I lie here thinking of the money that will be wasted on me, money that could be used by my family for constructive purposes.
>
> I had a happy childhood and a wonderful life. I spent nearly fifty years with a great husband and we raised a fine son.
>
> The doctors tell me I will have some "good" weeks when I recover from the surgery,

> perhaps several, but the cancer has gone too far and I cannot survive. When the pain becomes unbearable, I dearly wish the law would permit some kindly doctor to put me to sleep.
>
> The best I can do now is to put my request in writing (and I will surely do so) asking that no extraordinary measures be taken to keep me alive. I will permit no further surgery or medication except pain-killers.

"Be sure to let your family know exactly how you feel," the columnist counseled. "Too many terminally ill patients do not discuss this subject with their loved ones—and they should—openly and honestly. It can be a great release of tension for all concerned."

Dr. Nancy L. Caroline recently wrote an article for *The New Physician* in which she related her experiences in caring for a 78-year-old Jewish patient suffering from a terminal illness. The man watched a medical team vainly work for an hour on a patient who had gone into cardiac arrest in the bed next to his own. Before Dr. Caroline left the room, he said, "Don't ever do that to me! I want you should promise you'll never do that to me."

Although the promise was extracted, doctors later took extraordinary measures when this once-proud man went into congestive heart failure. "Swiftly," says Dr. Caroline, "the house staff swung into the practiced and coordinated action of acute care: morphine, oxygen, IPPB, tourniquets, digitalis, diuretics."

When none of these measures produced the desired medical response, the patient was intubated and hooked up to a ventilator. A cardiac monitor was attached to his chest.

"But you promised . . . " was all he could say.

Sometime late that night, he awakened and switched off the ventilator. The nurses found him several hours later and Dr. Caroline was called to pronounce him dead.

"The room was silent when I entered," she says. "The ventilator issued no rush of air, the monitor tracked a straight line, the suction was shut off. . . . The patient lay absolutely still. . . . On the bedside table I found a note, scrawled in an uneven hand: 'Death is not the enemy, doctor. Inhumanity is.' "

It had been written by a man who above all else wanted to be remembered as a *mensch*.

Earlier, when Dr. Caroline had first met him, she had been attracted by his candor and grasp of the medical situation.

"I'm dying," he said.

"Don't be silly."

"What's silly about dying?"

"Nothing. But it's not allowed. You are in a hospital, a university hospital, equipped with all the latest technology. Here you must get well."

"My time has come."

"Time is measured differently here."

"What do you understand about time?" the old man asked. "Wait until you are 78 years old and tired and alone and have a pain in your belly. Now, I'm dying. Okay. I'm not complaining. I'm old and tired and have seen enough of life, believe me. But still I want to be a man, not a vegetable that someone comes and waters every day."

Such accounts have led the medical profession to reevaluate its role in the care of the dying. Often doctors and nurses are beginning to deal realistically with their own problems of denial and defeat in facing death. They also are beginning to question whether the terminally ill themselves seek an elusive cure or merely a palliative for physical and emotional suffering.

One development which has sparked widespread interest in the medical world—and particularly in the United States—was the opening in 1967 of St. Christopher's Hospice in the working class Sydenham section of southeast London. Established under the auspices of a nondenominational religious foundation, this five-story, window-wrapped hospital specializes in the care of terminal cancer patients. But 10 percent of the 54 beds are reserved for others needing long-term treatment, usually neurological illnesses.

In that way, doctors and nurses can look the terminal patient straight in the eye and tell him truthfully, "Not everyone comes here to die." Some do leave St. Christopher's to return home.

Dr. Cicely Saunders, staff head, operates on the principle that a person's last days should be as pleasant and comfortable as possible. Therefore, extraordinary medical measures are out. Favorite foods, pastimes, and family members are in. Even grandchildren are permitted to visit a dying patient.

At St. Christopher's, even staff roles are diffused. "Anybody can love," says Dr. Robert E. Neale, a Union Theological Seminary professor who participated in an internship program there. "The right person at the right time does what is needed. Loving cuts across categories."

Moreover, St. Christopher's places the emphasis on the relief of pain—not on curing the hopeless case. Therefore, it has introduced practices which might shock many American Christians. For example, patients are permitted to use alcohol. Dr. Neale recalls one mobile gentleman "who walked to the local pub every morning and returned for the afternoon to sleep it off.

"All this is not to imply that dying at the hospice is participation in a drunken brawl," he says, "but that alcohol is perceived as a physiological, psychological, and social support. Families do enjoy a drink together."

Even more controversial is the use of heroin to head off pain and dispel the sense of gloom and depression so often seen in terminal cases. "The principle of anticipating pain and preventing rather than alleviating it," says Dr. Neale, "leads to use of low and frequent dosages."

Dr. Saunders observed that in American hospitals patients dying of cancer are usually "either in pain or 'slugged,' that is, practically knocked out with pain killers." In the typical American practice, she says, the patient is made to wait until the pain becomes unbearable. Then he is given too big a dose of drugs, a practice St. Christopher's seeks to avoid. In addition, often there is too long a gap between drug doses to kill the pain. The hospice attempts to rectify this out of compassion both to the patient and his family.

However, in spite of its highly unusual drug program, St. Christopher's is a religious institution, and Christianity plays a vital role in its operation. "The atmosphere . . . is religious," says Dr. Neale. "What the patients and staff catch . . . is the gentle persuasion that, somehow, everything is all right. To die is not to be abandoned but to be remembered by the living and taken up into God's arms."

Herself a devout Christian, Dr. Saunders conceives of St. Christopher's fulfilling Christ's plea to His disciples in the garden of Gethsemane: "Wait with Me." She says, "We don't preach at people, but we are Christians and believe in the resurrection. Death is not the end."

Like any other institution, St. Christopher's has its share of critics, nor does it presume to provide a perfect panacea for life's most traumatic moment. All that it can offer is another option for those who wish to spend their last days free of tubes and technology—and in the company of those who really care.

Reflecting upon his experiences at St. Christopher's, Dr. Neale recalled that when Goethe was about to die he cried: "Light, the world needs more light." However, when Unamuno heard this many years later, he was moved to write: "No,

Goethe was wrong. What he should have said was 'Warmth, the world needs more warmth.' We shall not die from the dark, but from the cold."

In its own unique way, St. Christopher's Hospice somehow tries to provide both light and warmth.

3. Where There's a Will

PAUL AND PEGGY MARTIN were both in their thirties when Paul was killed in an airplane crash. Peggy discovered that, although her husband had drawn up a will before their marriage, it was now out of date. As a result, the bulk of his estate went to his well-to-do parents, leaving Peggy and her two children with virtually nothing.

Jim and Irene Swanson felt they didn't need wills because they had only a small estate and all their financial assets were in joint ownership. However, when Jim died, Irene discovered their small holdings were enough to require her to pay an estate tax, which could have been substantially reduced had they discussed their estate with an attorney.

George and Sally Landers took a second honeymoon, leaving their two boys, nine and eleven, at summer camp. When they were killed in a highway accident, the court placed the youngsters in the custody of a close relative who shared none of the Landerses' values. This could have been easily avoided if they had not accepted the fallacious notion that joint ownership of property takes care of everything.

Betty Addington lost her husband when all three of their children were small. One child was seriously mentally retarded and probably would need close supervision for the remainder of his life. However, when Betty herself died without a will, the youngsters received equal shares of the estate, simply because Betty had failed to make special provision for her handicapped child.

Another drawback of this do-it-yourself age lies in the fact that many people think that they can write their own wills. To do so, however, is like playing Russian roulette, since the needs of each family differ, as do the laws of the various states. Therefore, it is vital to engage a competent attorney. It costs little, and it can save you much—both in terms of money and mental anguish!

Dwight E. Newbey, an executive of the United Methodist Board of Discipleship, laments the fact that so few pastors discuss the benefits of a will with young couples during premarital counseling. "The reason the minister fails to mention this necessity is that he has very little knowledge concerning wills," says Dr. Newbey. "And, further, he is probably one of the roughly 42 percent of ministers who do not themselves have wills."

During the first ten years of marriage, he says,

there is little likelihood that anyone will impress upon a young couple the need for a valid will. Yet, it is during this period that they likely will become parents and, in the event of death, will face unnecessary heartache.

Moreover, few couples ever consider that the unexpected death of the breadwinner can have a disastrous effect upon a family's standard of living, especially when any of the children are under 21. "During the years of child-rearing, financial demands increase for the couple who are now approaching a peak both in earnings and expenditures," Dr. Newbey observes. "It is possible that both of the parents are working and the total income is substantial." But with the breadwinner's death, he adds, comes the financial shock. Even if the widow herself is working, her earnings are often insufficient to keep up the same standard of living. And this sobering fact, of course, demands a totally different life-style.

Or take the case of a couple who die intestate *after* their children have reached maturity. In the eyes of the law, the children have an absolute right to dispose of, or even squander, any inheritance as they see fit. When the father precedes his wife in death, a will can make certain that his spouse will inherit his entire estate. Or, conditions permitting, he can make specific bequests to his children, depending upon their ages and individual needs.

Many couples have visualized those years which they can spend together, free of earlier financial responsibilities. But those dreams can be shattered for a surviving spouse when a will does not exist. Regardless of age, the children will share in the estate of a father who dies intestate. Meanwhile, the wife may have to face the burden of trying to carve out a new life, often without an adequate amount of money.

A will is also crucial for single people. Above all, it permits you alone to decide how to dispose of your earthly possessions following your death. Unfortunately, however, many believe that this important step can be put off until some elusive tomorrow. Life is fragile, and those who procrastinate are more often than not among the one million Americans who die of cardiovascular disease alone each year. In the end, however, it is their families who suffer the most.

A nationwide tax publication recently reported that the seven out of eight people who die intestate pump $96 million into the probate courts each week. "This means not only extra cost," says World Vision stewardship director Ron Arnold, "but distribution is made according to state law rather than the desires of the deceased. Each year millions of dollars are wasted in unnecessary expenses because people fail in their obligation to God and family."

If any or all of these arguments are convincing, then your next step is to engage an attorney in your state of legal residence to draft a will (or wills) which meet the particular needs of your family. Before doing so, however, you might like to obtain some of the excellent materials on wills and estates which are available from several major religious organizations. Among others, World Vision and the United Presbyterian Foundation provide extremely helpful counseling resources.* All are free of charge.

Meanwhile, as Ron Arnold points out, your estate can be broken down into three components:

ASSETS
(What You Own)

LIABILITIES
(What You Owe)

SURPLUS
(What You Have Left)

Once you make a systematic effort to list all of your assets, you'll be surprised at how much wealthier you are than you thought. For your assets include not only savings but insurance policies, investments, real estate, all your personal effects from your car to your furniture, and any inheritance you may have received.

However, when death strikes, many are surprised to learn just how interested the tax collector is in their small estate. In fact, banks are generally required by tax authorities to freeze all accounts

* The United Presbyterian Foundation, 475 Riverside Drive, New York, NY 10027, offers a free personal record book, which it advises families to update regularly. World Vision International, 919 West Huntington Drive, Monrovia, CA 91016, provides an excellent guide, "God's Will and My Will."

and safety deposit boxes temporarily until a release is obtained assuring them that all applicable taxes will be paid. Therefore, unless a spouse has adequate cash on hand or a separate bank account in his or her own name, he or she may have difficulty in obtaining money to pay pressing bills at the time of a death.

In some states, trust accounts rather than joint accounts are recommended to meet such emergencies. In this case, one account could read, "John Jones in trust for Mary Jones," while the other would be in the name of Mary Jones, "in trust for John Jones." Again, however, this is an instance in which it is wise to seek professional counsel in your own state of legal residence.

One source of ready cash is to be found in your insurance policies, provided they have *not* been locked away in your safety deposit box. Such policies generally do not come under a state's probate laws. However, you should keep a handy record of the policy numbers, the insurance companies, and the names of the beneficiaries. A copy of this information should then be placed in the hands of the executor of your estate, along with information as to where the policies are located.

Don't dismiss any policy as worthless, for often a so-called "lapsed" policy may provide some death benefit through continuing extended term coverage. Also, don't discount limited benefit policies you received from a union, social organization, or travel club.

In a day of rising medical costs, it is important to

keep a record of your surgical and hospitalization policies, both those provided by your employer and those purchased privately. Also don't forget any Social Security or pension benefits to which you are entitled. Your family may also be eligible for other financial help at the time of your death from a union, fraternal organization, a veterans group, etc.

The need for up-to-date records is also necessary in the case of your investments. Valuable rights are often lost to survivors simply because they cannot locate stocks and bonds purchased by the deceased, including those U.S. Saving (war) bonds. For those who have created trust funds, it will be further necessary for your attorney and executor to quickly pinpoint the following:

The name(s) in which thc trust(s) was established.

The date and location of the trust agreement.

The names of the trustees and that of the attorney who originally drafted the agreement.

Whether you yourself are a beneficiary under a trust established by someone else in the past, and whether your heirs are eligible for benefits under such prior agreements.

Thousands of checking and savings accounts go unclaimed every year because deceased depositors simply failed to alert their loved ones to their existence. Not only may such accounts be subjected to a loss of interest after a specified period, but unclaimed deposits ultimately go into the state's coffers rather than to loved ones who may badly need the money. Therefore, although all accounts are temporarily frozen at death, it is imperative that a record be kept of their numbers and locations. Also, someone should know the location of the deposit books.

For most middle-class families, however, their house represents a substantial part of any estate. At the time of death, your attorney will want to know who, if anyone, holds a mortgage on the property. He will further require the deed, title abstract, and title insurance policy, surveys, closing statement, insurance policies, tax receipts, and any other pertinent data. Moreover, similar information will be needed when an individual or couple owns a business or other property, such as a farm or undeveloped land. In addition, those who hold leases or are bound by them should have such documents readily available in case of death.

As to tax advantages on real estate holdings, a serious question is whether a couple should hold such assets in joint ownership or as "tenants in common." It's a fine legal distinction, but is most crucial and its proper resolution could save you money. It is a matter to settle with the aid of an attorney versed in the subject.

Meanwhile, both the tax collector and family members will be interested in a person's other tangible assets or personal effects. Such items may include an automobile, television set, stereo, piano, organ, furniture, appliances, jewelry, books, art work, antiques, and heirlooms. Many a nasty family squabble could have been avoided if only the individual had designated the disposition of such assets. Ask your attorney about the best way to do this.

So much for assets. Now let's look at your liabilities.

In most wills, a standard provision states: "I direct that all my just debts be paid as soon as practicable after my decease." Those "just debts" include charge accounts, loans, contracts, terminal medical expenses, funeral costs, and, of course, Uncle Sam. One's creditors hold priority in the settlement of any estate, and probate court determinations always take them into account.

In an age of spiraling medical costs, a family can soften the financial blow of a serious and/or extended illness by participating in a voluntary insurance plan which covers the charges of both the doctor and the hospital. If your employer does not provide such protection, a separate major medical policy should be obtained to meet expenses above and beyond your other doctor-hospital insurance.

Blue Cross—Blue Shield subscribers should remember that, upon reaching age 65, they are eligible for Senior Care, which provides the amount deductible under Medicare—a deductible amount that has been steadily rising over the years.

Moreover, no family can ever predict if it will be faced with a so-called "catastrophic illness" which could involve expenses that only the wealthy could ever hope to bear. If such a tragedy should occur, it is wise to investigate the possibility of receiving total disability benefits under the Medicare program benefits which, in such cases, are available to those under 65 years of age.

The bereaved can be spared a great deal of unnecessary anguish if certain steps are taken before a death occurs. Here are some of the questions to be resolved:

> Has a decision been made as to whether the body will be buried or cremated?
>
> If burial is preferred, has the family selected and paid for a plot in the cemetery of its choice?
>
> If so, where is the deed located? Is perpetual care to be provided?
>
> Has the family met with a local funeral director to discuss funeral arrangements, remembering that all costs will reflect prevailing prices at the time a death actually occurs?

Again, by taking these simple steps, survivors can sometimes be spared an additional burden—and often needless costs—at a time when they are least able to face such questions.

However, it should be kept in mind that the survivors, for emotional and psychological reasons, need to be involved to some degree. They should also be able to alter instructions or recommendations in the case of a pre-arranged funeral that would prove difficult, ill-advised or guilt-producing for them.

Christians also can turn to a favorite religious or charitable organization for guidance in tax matters that will later arise at the time of death. However, beyond the services offered by a reputable group, professional tax counsel can be extremely valuable in planning one's estate and in formulating the terms of a will. Such advice can often save a family a considerable amount that would otherwise go to the state and federal governments.

Here are various taxes which can be levied against an estate:

INCOME TAX returns must be filed for a decedent if his or her income exceeded the minimum statutory exemption during the year the death occurred. However, careful planning can minimize such taxes through gifts, trusts, and annuities.

ESTATE TAXES are levied by the federal government and most states, if a person's wealth exceeds a specified amount. The statutes define a taxable estate in terms of the gross estate less funeral expenses, administrative costs, debts, gifts to religious and charitable organizations, an individual exemption and, where applicable, a marital deduction.

GIFT TAXES are computed in various ways. There

are no limitations on gifts to qualifying religious and charitable groups, but, in the case of gifts to individuals, there are both single and lifetime limitations. In addition to the state and federal incomes, estate and gift taxes, survivors must be prepared to pay those levies prescribed by state law, when estates exceed a certain net value.

At the secular level, the U.S. Supreme Court has ruled, in Gregory vs. Helvering, that "the legal right of a taxpayer to decrease the amount of what otherwise would be his taxes, or to altogether avoid them by means which the law permits, cannot be doubted." Moreover, the distinguished Justice Learned Hand said, in another landmark decision: "Anyone may so arrange his affairs that taxes shall be as low as possible; he is not bound to choose that pattern which will best pay the treasury; it is not even a patriotic duty to increase one's taxes."

The reasons for sound fiscal planning are even more compelling for the Christian. In admonishing His disciples to be good stewards of their earthly possessions, Jesus sadly observed that "the children of this world are in their generation wiser than the children of light" (Lk. 16:8).

"In other words," says World Vision executive vice president Ted W. Engstrom, "Jesus inferred that worldly people with their selfish motives were more clever in handling their money than Christians. Happily, this situation is changing."

Thanks to organizations such as World Vision International, Christians are beginning to recognize that they have a mandate to engage in sound stewardship practices. And that mandate is found in the following Biblical counsel:

> God exhorts us to be good stewards of the possessions He has entrusted to our care (Mt. 25:14-30).
>
> God expects us to carefully consider the distribution of our remaining estates according to *His will* (I Tim. 6:7; II Cor. 9:6-8).
>
> God promises to reward us with *heavenly* treasures if we honor Him with *earthly* treasures (Mt. 6:19-21).
>
> God instructs us to make provision for our dependents (I Tim. 5:8).
>
> God intends that we consider the laws of our country, including tax laws, in planning the settlement of our estates (Rom. 13:1-7).
>
> God entrusts the life-giving Gospel to us and requires us to be faithful in sharing it with others (I Cor. 4:1, 2).

Although these admonitions may have little effect on others, the Christian accepts them as a basis for determining how his surplus is to be divided after he has tallied his assets and, to the best of his knowledge, has deducted his liabilities. Of course, the first order of business is to make certain that one's dependents are properly cared for both in life and in death. The Bible declares:

> But anyone who won't care for his own relatives when they need help, especially those living in his own family, has no right to say he is a Christian. Such a person is worse than the heathen (I Tim. 5:8, *The Living Bible*).

Therefore, to assure the best possible care for survivors, the wise Christian will not only have a will, but he will see to it that it is updated as changes occur in his family. Sometimes it is only necessary to make an amendment or to add a codicil; on other occasions, a new will should be drafted. Moreover, competent professional counsel can advise the Christian on the best means of utilizing the complex provisions of the tax laws to their fullest advantage.

For example, let's look at some provisions which are well known to the wealthy but often overlooked by middle-class couples who have little knowledge of their real net worth.

If the wife's income or other assets are minimal, the husband can transfer cash, securities, or other property worth up to $6,000 a year to her as a tax-free gift. The same privilege holds true for the wife if the financial situation is reversed. In addition, parents can make tax-free gifts annually to their children. Moreover, federal law provides for a $30,000 lifetime gift exemption for each person—exclusive of those gifts up to $3,000 made on an annual basis.

Whether these provisions should be utilized, however, depends upon a number of factors. Your attorney should advise you on this point.

Federal estate taxes are levied on estates of more than $60,000 for the single taxpayer, or double that amount for married couples. Again, you should seek the counsel of a qualified attorney.

In exploring these possibilities, you'll probably find that you're worth far more than you ever dreamed possible, once you've tallied up all of your assets.

Therefore, Christians do have the added obligation—or privilege—to remember God's will in drafting their own last will and testament. Paul wrote:

> Let a man so account of us, as of the ministers of Christ, and stewards of the mysteries of God. Moreover it is required in stewards, that a man be found faithful (I Cor. 4:1, 2).

Our faithfulness as "stewards of the mysteries of God" can be measured, in no small degree, as we make provision to transfer in life or at death unneeded savings, insurance policies, real estate, and/or other personal property to the cause of Jesus Christ in a lost and needy world. To assist Christians in their estate planning, religious organizations can often provide valuable information on various types of bequests, ranging from trust funds to annuities, which not only help others but provide income and/or tax savings for our own families.

Dr. Paul A. Qualben, director of psychiatry at Lutheran Medical Center, Brooklyn, New York, has introduced a new dimension of Christian stewardship with a uniquely modern ring. An ordained Lutheran pastor as well as a practicing psychiatrist, Dr. Qualben notes that this added option resulted from the dramatic advances in medical science. Because of these advances, he says, Christians can now offer unto the Lord not only their time, talents and treasures—but their tissue as well.

"In the New Testament," he observes, "the imagery of Christ shedding His blood for mankind is used repeatedly. Blood, of course, is a tissue. The picture in the Scriptures is that of Christ giving Himself totally—spiritually and physically—for a sinful world."

Thanks to medical science, Christians can now follow their Lord in donating their blood during their lifetimes—and, at death, they can offer hope to the blind, the kidney and cardiac patient, and to those who suffer from diseases of the spleen, liver, pancreas, lungs, bone marrow, and skin. Even secretions from the endocrine organs, although not transplanted themselves, can offer new life to some other human being.

Under provisions of the 1968 Uniform Anatomical Gift Act, any person 18 years or older of sound mind can normally donate all or part of his body for medical purposes. His wishes take priority over those of his survivors and can be documented by any written instrument signed by the donor and witnessed by two other persons. Since time is frequently of the essence, the American Medical Association has prepared a uniform donor card which the individual may carry at all times. This card may save another life.*

As Norman M. Lobsenz has pointed out, individuals often have the opportunity to permit doctors to perform autopsies on a loved one who has just died. By granting such permission, he says, medical science is aided in the following ways:

> Autopsies reveal pathological problems and changes detected in no other way.
>
> Autopsies indicate the effectiveness of new weapons against disease.
>
> Autopsies provide a double check on diagnoses.
>
> And, in some instances, autopsies can actually ease the burden of grief for a bereaved family.

Ultimately, the choice is yours alone as to what is to be done both with your earthly treasure and your physical remains. But that choice must be guided by a prayerful consideration of Christian stewardship and wise planning in advance. Moreover, it is your decision alone as to who will best serve as the guardian of your children, and the attorney and executor of your estate, provided you have drafted a legal and

*A replica of the AMA Uniform Donor Card is appended in the back of the book.

up-to-date will. Since your executor will act as business manager in the settlement of your estate, you should take these facts into consideration:

> Assemble in advance all of the documents he will need to carry out his task efficiently: data on savings, investments, insurance, real estate, tax returns, birth and marriage certificates, naturalization papers, military serial number, discharge papers, the deed to your cemetery plot, as well as any other information which can also aid your attorney, funeral director and pastor.
>
> Suggest to your executor that he obtain a sufficient number of copies of the death certificate to meet the requirements of federal and state tax authorities, the Veterans Administration, insurance companies, the union, and any other source of financial benefits to which your survivors may be entitled.
>
> Think about the possibility of selecting as your executor someone who is thoroughly competent but younger than yourself. Contemporaries often precede one in death.

If you have taken care of all of these matters, then both you and your loved ones can rest a bit easier. And, in a very real sense, it can be said at the appropriate time that: "He being dead yet speaketh" (Heb. 11:4).

4. The Choice Is Yours

ONE WELL-KNOWN COLUMNIST has opined that he fears that most people "are condemned to live."

"Prices are so outrageous that I have just discovered to my sorrow," he writes, "that I can no longer afford to die. The good old $500 funeral has gone with the cadaver."

However, he did hold out some hope for people who join organizations such as the Neptune Society of California. "The cost of membership is $25 a couple," he notes, "and it doesn't matter which one decides to move out first. The Neptunes, for an additional $250, will cremate the remains and dump the ashes at sea from an ornate urn. Don't knock it unless you've tried it."

But this kind of macabre humor generally fails to draw a laugh from many funeral directors, especially after they have read in the news columns of the same paper: "If you don't have $960, you can't afford to die." That was the average price cited by a New York State commission for the cheapest funeral offered by members of the New York State Funeral Directors Association in 1974. Actually, the national average was somewhat lower.

However, what particularly galls the funeral director are the charges of price fixing, massive price gouging, and deceptive billing. In addition, it has been claimed that comparison shopping for funerals is extremely difficult.

"I don't know anyone who is going to bargain with a funeral director over money, or price different funeral homes after his mother or father has died," one legislator told the press. "The consumer is at the mercy of the funeral director, and the markups on caskets and services are tremendous."

"The high cost of funerals," said another well-known columnist, "obviously is one key reason increasing numbers of Americans are opting for cremation or for bequeathing their bodies to medical schools (though the body must still either be buried or cremated afterward) or for prearranged, inexpensive memorial society funeral packages."

However, she offered some other hints for price-conscious families. She suggested that readers determine whether a body can be delivered directly to a crematorium by "private individuals or ambulance services." If the body is cremated some distance from home, she noted, "the container with the ashes can be mailed home by parcel post or carried in a suitcase."

Although most Americans cringe at such suggestions, they have nonetheless been influenced by the continual diatribe against the funeral profession. What, then, are the facts about the so-called "high cost of dying"?

"Only a few problems involving the services of funeral directors, cemeteries, and monument makers are brought to the attention of Better Business Bureaus," according to a survey conducted by the BBB's national association. At the same time, the survey and other studies noted that, paradoxically, there exists "a noticeable degree of public suspicion and criticism of funeral directors and allied groups." Two explanations were offered for this "unusual situation":

1. Widespread public ignorance and misunderstanding of the many services performed by these groups.
2. Questionable advertising, high-pressure sales tactics, and serious malpractices by a small minority such as exists on the fringe of any business or profession.

The latter, said the BBB survey, "victimize bereaved families and create public distrust out of all proportion to their numbers."

But this is enough to make organizations such as the National Funeral Directors Association and the National Selected Morticians take positive steps to root out this fringe from their numbers. For example, the following Code of Good Funeral Practice is subscribed to by every member of the second professional body:

To provide the public with information about funerals, including prices, and about the functions, services, and responsibilities of funeral directors.

To afford a continuing opportunity to all persons to discuss or arrange funerals in advance.

To make funerals available in as wide a range of price categories as necessary to meet the need of all segments of the community, and affirmatively to extend to everyone the right of inspecting and freely considering all of them.

To quote conspicuously in writing the charges for every funeral offered; to identify clearly the services, facilities, equipment, and merchandise included in such quotations; and to follow a policy of reasonable adjustment when less than the quoted offering is utilized.

To furnish to each family, at the time funeral arrangements are made, a written memorandum of charges and to make no additional charge without the approval of the purchaser.

To make no representation, written or oral, which may be false or misleading, and to apply a standard of total honesty in all dealings.

To respect all faiths, creeds and customs, and

to give full effect to the role of the clergy.

To maintain a qualified and competent staff, complete facilities and suitable equipment required for comprehensive funeral service.

To assure those we serve the right of personal choice and decision in making funeral arrangements.

To be responsive to the needs of the poor, serving them within their means.

This statement may help to alleviate some suspicions of price fixing, massive price gouging, deceptive billing, and the alleged inability of the public to compare prices and services offered by various funeral homes. But the question remains whether most members of the funeral profession live up to so high a code of professional conduct. Just what can a bereaved family expect from a local funeral director?

First, the funeral profession has been hit by inflation. Therefore, if they are to remain in business, funeral directors must pass on these higher costs to the consumer. But no profession has been more determined to hold the price line within reasonable limits.* Many urban funeral directors have found it prohibitive to purchase, maintain, and operate their own limousines, hearses, and flower cars, so some

*According to a 1974 fact card published by the NFDA, in the period between 1967 and 1974 the cost of living went up 55.4% while the cost of adult funerals increased only 39.3%.

liveries have been formed to hold down costs and yet provide service to funeral homes in a given area, a move reflected in the consumer's final bill.

But such economy moves fail to answer the question: What will it cost today to provide a dignified funeral for a loved one? The answer depends upon several factors.

Howard C. Raether, executive director of the National Funeral Directors Association, points out that funeral practices differ throughout the country. "A custom in California may seem strange in Vermont," he observes. "There is no one prescribed form of the funeral. The funeral which is arranged should be the one which best meets the needs of those who survive."

This means two things: First, costs vary in different sections of the country. In rural Pennsylvania, the deceased's pallbearers will probably be his lifelong friends and neighbors, but in New York City they will all be union members.

Jurisdictional agreements decree that Teamster members who drive the hearses and limousines have priority over the unionized pallbearers. Moreover, the number of pallbearers is determined by strict contract negotiations. In addition, costs can vary widely for the opening of the grave. Various cemeteries have their own rate schedules, but the hour and day of the week will determine whether laborers are entitled to overtime pay. Apart from such factors, the funeral cost will be determined by the merchandise and the services required by the family.

There is absolute consensus among all reputable funeral directors that it is false to charge that bereaved families are at their mercy. While many families make arrangements in advance, others *do* compare prices after a death has occurred. Recently a funeral director who serves as a rural coroner was called to the scene of a highway accident to pronounce a passenger's death. The body was removed by a competitor.

Many families are ill-equipped at the time of a death to compare funeral services, but arrangements do not have to be made immediately. In fact, autopsies may hold up the release of a body and, invariably, the first viewing is never held until the following day.

Funeral directors generally do not like to discuss arrangements by telephone. "I personally have found over the years," says one director, "that people have so many different ideas as to what constitutes a dignified funeral that making arrangements by phone is never completely satisfactory to the family. Usually there are three or four people who are directly concerned. And if one person does make the arrangements by phone, other members of the family later complain that their wishes were not considered."

To avoid such problems, many people discuss arrangements with a funeral director prior to the time of death. "Actually," says Howard Raether, "there are almost as many explanations for prearranging funerals as there are people requesting them." For example, some without families want to make certain that funeral arrangements will meet their personal beliefs, standards, and life-style. Others feel a responsibility to assist survivors by arranging approximate funeral and burial-cost guidelines.

"Still others have moved to distant places or maintain both summer and winter residences," he adds. "They may want to make sure that certain recommendations are heeded as to where the funeral and burial or other final dispositions will take place."

Raether cautions that there are important factors to consider in the prearranging and prefinancing of funerals:

Review the possible effect on survivors.

Approach realistically the logic and economics of planning now what might not take place for many years.

Keep in mind that the selection of a funeral director or a funeral home as well as burial merchandise for use at a future indeterminable time must, of necessity, be on a tentative basis.

Remember, too, that money paid in advance of need for funeral services and merchandise, including burial vaults, is governed by law in most states.

Where state law does not govern prearranged

funerals, the NFDA executive secretary recommends that "the prepaid funeral agreement include the provision for a trust fund with the person making the payment maintaining control of the account. The fund should include all money paid in advance of need for services and merchandise, including burial vaults," he advises. "The agreement should also entitle the person in control of the trust to the interest earned with the option of applying it to the principal to offset any increased inflationary costs. Such persons making the payment should retain the right to terminate the contract at any time without forfeiture of any of the funds paid or earnings accrued."

Of course, this means that a person cannot expect to pay today's prices for a funeral which might not take place for many years. Once one of New York City's largest funeral establishments did attempt to guarantee price stability without regard to inflation to persons prefinancing funeral arrangements. This firm is no longer in business!

Families should be prepared to pay for four separate and distinct categories of charges for a traditional funeral: (1) those of the funeral director, including professional services, use of facilities, and the casket and vault selected; (2) the cemetery or cremation charges; (3) the cost of monument or marker; and (4) miscellaneous expenses such as honorarium for the clergyman, flowers, newspaper notices, etc.

Although many do not formally make funeral arrangements until death strikes, the majority have some notion as to which funeral director would be called because:

1. They have come to know and respect a particular funeral director.

2. They have been impressed by the professional conduct and services offered by a particular firm while attending funerals.

Therefore, a man's reputation is his best advertisement.

Families want to know that they are dealing with people who are thoroughly professional, a fact demonstrated by the rigorous training of today's funeral director. In general, the professional curriculum for aspiring directors consists of three areas of study:

Basic and health sciences including anatomy, chemistry, bacteriology, pathology, hygiene, and public health.

Funeral service arts and sciences consisting of embalming and restorative art.

Funeral service administration involving accounting, funeral law, funeral principles, psychology, directing, and management.

After this study is completed, the student must take the state and/or national board exams. Then he must take a resident training program, varying in length from one to three years. If he decides to strike out on his own, he will be aware that according to the NFDA the investment range in 1973 for funeral homes averaged $113,224 for those conducting less than 100 funerals a year, and $513,200 for those holding more than 300 services.

Such large investments have been the target of critics, but most families consider a funeral home partially on the basis of its facilities. They seek those firms which can provide sufficient room for funeral services as well as a pleasing decor.

Once established, the new funeral director is in a stable profession. "The average firm has been in the community 45 years," says sociologist Robert C. Slater. "It is becoming common for funeral homes to have a history of 75-100 years of service. Some are in the fourth generation of the family. This is evidence of both the stability of the funeral home within the community it serves and of the personnel serving the firm."

Such factors cannot help but loom large in any objective study of funeral costs. Consider that attorneys are seldom available at night or on weekends, and few doctors are willing to make house calls. But, with few exceptions, the funeral director is at your service 24 hours a day, 365 days a year. Death never takes a holiday nor does it conform to prescribed working hours.

Consequently, as Howard Raether observes, it is completely erroneous to judge funeral costs in terms of tangible goods. "On the average," he says, "the merchandise provided by a funeral director amounts to about 20 percent of his total cost in providing a funeral service. The casket is not the funeral. Nor is the funeral the casket."

Unfortunately, however, many funeral directors have contributed to this erroneous notion by failing to explain their pricing practices adequately to the general public. The four most widely used accounting methods are:

1. The single unit or standard method which quotes a single funeral price, including professional services, use of the facilities, and the casket;

2. The bi-unit method which breaks down charges into two basic figures: the casket price, and the cost for professional services and the use of facilities;

3. The tri-unit method which shows the charges for, first of all, the professional services, secondly the use of facilities and equipment, and thirdly the casket;

4. The functional or itemized method which lists the prices for the various facets of the funeral, including professional services, the facilities and equipment, the casket and other merchandise.

In New York State, funeral directors are required

by law to provide families with a statement of all charges. "These are *not* estimates," a spokesman emphasizes. "The statement rather represents the exact charges based upon the services requested by the family." This means that cost differences between similar funerals will depend largely upon two factors: (1) The exact services ordered, and (2) the difference in overhead among funeral homes.

But let's take a look at the funeral director at work. He enters the picture after he has received word of a death from a clergyman, loved one, or a close friend. This initial call may come at any hour, but it will bring him immediately.

However, before a removal can take place, he must obtain certain vital information before he can begin his work. Such data may be required by state law and/or local ordinance. Many cities and counties prohibit the removal of the body until a permit or death certificate has been signed by an attending physician, coroner, or medical examiner. In any case, a death certificate must ultimately be obtained by the funeral director. When a physician has not been in attendance, this certificate may be signed by the coroner or medical examiner, especially in accident, violence, or questionable death cases. The director must also obtain a burial permit. And, in some areas, permission must be secured to embalm a body which is to be cremated.

But that's not all. Since many Americans now are buried in a location other than the place of death, the director must obtain a transit permit before he can move a body across state lines. Some states even require a temporary removal permit for interstate transfers outside the registration district in which the death occurred. The director himself generally assumes full responsibility for the proper completion and filing of these various forms, for it isn't a job for a novice.

After the initial legal requirements have been observed, the director will remove the body to the funeral home and then arrange to meet the family to work out other details. One of the first matters to be resolved is the time and place of the funeral service. The family's wishes will have to coincide with the clergyman's schedule.

After determining the family's wishes regarding interment, entombment, or cremation, the director will immediately notify the appropriate cemetery or crematorium, since regulations governing the time of final dispositions are growing more stringent in many localities. If someone is to be buried on a family plot, the survivors will have to produce the deed and determine the exact location. When a gravesite has not been purchased in advance, the family must acquire a plot.

Often, funeral directors have absolutely no connection with cemeteries, and in some states are forbidden by law to make a profit from a gravesite. In New York, nonsectarian cemeteries are under the jurisdiction of a state agency, while those maintained by various faiths are directly controlled by religious authorities.

An increasing number of Americans die in one area and are to be buried in a different section of the country. Therefore, several important and complicated decisions must be made. First is the matter of transportation. Generally airlines offer more convenient and economical service than railroads when long distances are involved. However, it is often feasible to use the director's transportation facilities when interment is less than 200 miles away.

In many instances, however, the transfer of a body demands the services of more than one funeral home. This raises the question of "partial service pricing," for which the National Funeral Directors Association has adopted the following canon in its Code of Professional Practice:

> When death occurs in a place other than where the funeral and/or burial are to take place, most times the services of two funeral directors are necessary. Under such circumstances the family should not pay for a complete service both where death occurred and also where the burial or cremation is held.
>
> The forwarding funeral director should make an allowance or adjustment for those of his services not required and should notify the receiving funeral director thereof. Likewise the receiving funeral director should not charge the family for the services already provided by the forwarding funeral director unless there is a duplication thereof desired by the family.
>
> The family should pay for only one complete

service plus any additional charges incurred because the place of death and the place of final disposition require the services of two funeral firms.

Meanwhile, many other decisions are still to be made. The director will need to know about suitable clothing, wording the obituary, the selection of family flowers, the use of music, and the desire, if any, for rituals other than those conducted by the clergyman. Moreover, he will have to determine whether the family intends to name and use friends of the deceased as pallbearers wherever permissible. He also will settle transportation: vehicles required from the livery, as well as the anticipated number of private cars in the funeral cortege.

The family will be asked to decide on a casket. In many instances, they will simply be led into the director's display room to make their selection. In other cases, they will be shown photographs or three-dimensional color slides of available models and materials. The Casket Manufacturers' Association has found that various types of caskets tend to be favored in different parts of the country.

There are also regional preferences regarding the casket style. The most widely favored is the half-couch, which shows the body from the waist up, although some areas prefer the full-couch models, which permit the entire body to be viewed. A hinge-cap casket, similar to the half-couch, is also available. The family itself determines the style, construction, and price of the casket.

When the body is taken to the funeral home, it is carefully washed and embalmed. In some cases, embalming is required by law, especially when the body will be in transit, when death was caused by certain infectious diseases, or when the length of time between death and final disposition exceed a prescribed period.

The licensed staff will use its skills in the restorative arts to erase ravages of age, disease, and disfiguring accidents. Without these techniques, many families would be denied a final look at someone they loved. In unfortunate instances where these arts cannot correct extreme disfigurement, the director may have to recommend that the casket remain closed.

Once the body is placed in state, relatives and friends will be able to visit the funeral home. Although the viewing may be restricted to the afternoon and evening before the funeral service, this period is somctimes extended. Local custom dictates whether more friends attend the viewing or the funeral and committal rites.

As a general rule, funeral services are held on the third day following the death, barring weekends, holidays, and certain weather conditions. Again, religious and regional traditions determine whether services are conducted in the church or funeral home, or at both.*

At this point, the need for thoroughgoing professionalism becomes quite obvious. The funeral di-

*The role of the clergyman is covered in chapter 6.

rector has already prepared the body, obtained the selected casket and vault, and notified the cemetery or crematorium of the day and hour of final disposition. But he also has contacted the clergyman, notified the newspapers, arranged the flowers, and received callers.

On the day of the funeral, he will usher guests to their seats, organize the funeral cortege, and then perform one of the most difficult tasks of his profession: gently lead a spouse, parent, or child from the casket to a waiting limousine.

Although the casket is generally closed during church services, family members will always look for the last time at their deceased loved one. To reduce this trauma, the thoroughly professional funeral director never closes the casket in the family's presence. (The author has witnessed only two occasions in which this procedure was ignored. In both instances, loved ones broke into hysteria.) Rather, he waits until all are seated in the limousine. Then the body is moved into the hearse.

"The committal service provides as nothing else . . . does so graphically," says Paul E. Irion, a noted pastoral psychologist, "a symbolic demonstration that the kind of relationship which has existed between the mourner and the deceased is now at an end."

The grave will be filled by cemetery workmen after the participants have left the cemetery. Often the conscientious director will remain until the last burial detail has been completed. However, his work is far from over. "After the service, he assists the family in filing necessary claims for Social Security, veterans and union benefits, and insurance," says Howard Raether. "Often the funeral director serves a family for several months following a funeral until all matters and details are satisfactorily completed for the family." (I know of instances in which alert funeral directors have uncovered benefits of which families have been unaware. Such benefits often substantially reduce the financial burden for these bereaved families.)

Returning to funeral costs, in 1974, the Life Insurance Agency Management Association in *What Does She Do Now?* stated that the total cost of a funeral or alternative ranged between $550 and $3,000 with an average cost of $1,750.*

When the NFDA speaks of the average adult funeral, it refers to one for persons 15 years of age and older, as well as to the casket size required. However, about 20 percent of the funerals are for welfare recipients, children, and those requiring only partial-adult services. In these cases the cost was well below the average. Yet all of these figures include the cost of professional services, use of facilities, merchandise, and cash advances. To what do these advances or miscellaneous items refer?

The fact is that the burden would be much heavier to bear if the director did not free the family from many little financial details: advancing honoraria, obtaining copies of the death certificate, tipping cemetery workmen, and even paying turnpike

*See Appendix II for the average funeral charges per firm for adults in 1973.

tolls for the entire funeral procession, whenever necessary.

Critics of funeral practices often link the director with charges not at all involved with his profession from which he does not personally benefit, including costs connected with interment, cremation, and permanent memorials. "In most cemeteries the cost of an individual grave ranges from about $75 to $350," an NFDA survey found. "Costs of opening and closing the grave range from $50 to $250. Prices for individual crypts in indoor mausolea start at about $600. Outside garden crypts begin at about $350."

As for cemetery markers and monuments, there is a wide range of prices based upon size, material, design, and craftsmanship. Most cemeteries have rules regulating the size and type of such memorials. There may even be regulations regarding the use of fresh and/or artificial flowers.

If a family favors cremation, it will spend between $35 to $150 for final disposal. In addition, bronze urns for the remains will cost from $50 to more than $250. These urns may then be placed in columbaria niches, which range in price from $35 to $750, depending upon size, location, and quality.

Inflation and other variables can radically alter the overall costs involved in a traditional funeral. It may cost considerably more than the highest estimated amount to open and close a grave, particularly when union help is required. A lot would then depend upon the time and day of the committal rites.

In an effort to trim down funeral costs, other alternatives have been suggested. Among these are memorial societies (although these serve merely as mediators between the bereaved family and the funeral director), and labor union and cooperative funeral homes. Although the latter are few in number, about 100 memorial societies are in about as many United States cities. All stress simplicity and dignity and suggest that families consider the body's immediate disposition with a memorial service to be held later without the body present. One society's brochure suggests "that ostentatious burial practices such as costly caskets, rented limousines, and large floral displays be eliminated."

To join a memorial society, a variable membership fee is paid for literature on options at death, preplanning forms, and a list of funeral directors who support the concept and offer a variety of options. However, the officers and staffs of these organizations are not licensed to conduct funerals or to make funeral arrangements. They act largely in a referral capacity.

Memorial societies have their own share of critics. Geoffrey Gorer, a British anthropologist, dislikes the idea of memorial services after the final disposal of the body. "It would seem correct to state," he says, "that a society which denies mourning, and gives no ritual support to mourners, is thereby producing maladaptive and neurotic responses in a number of citizens."

Alfred A. Messer of Emory University is even more pointed. "Memorial services, held a couple of weeks after death, are for the birds—not for human beings,'' he insists. ''When there is a funeral, there should be a body there, and I think it should be an open casket. . . . When there is death, there should be a funeral. There is no association in people's minds between a memorial service and a man who died two weeks ago.''

The funeral profession itself contends that people should not have to pay money to join a memorial society just for literature and a price list. George Goodstein, a spokesman for the Metropolitan Funeral Directors and the New York State Funeral Directors Association, maintains that anyone can prearrange his or her funeral directly with a local firm which offers informed and sympathetic advice—not pamphlets and forms.

As the NFDA points out, community standards determine the funeral director's professional conduct. It is just poor business for a firm to provide services beyond the reach of particular families, or to become involved in practices which can only create ill will and/or legal action. After all, the director is a community member, and it is to the community that he must turn for support.

In all seriousness, a funeral is not unlike a trip abroad. An individual can shop for the cheapest tour, only to be sadly disappointed with the arrangements. Similarly, when a family selects a funeral director well known in the community, it will generally discover that the smallest detail has been anticipated and that family requests have been carried out to the letter.

"In my 35 years as a Christian minister," says one pastor, "I have yet to find a mortician, among the many I have known, who has high-pressured the bereaved into buying what they could not afford. To the contrary, I have known of some morticians who have talked people down to purchasing a less costly service."

William E. Gladstone, a great Christian and British statesman, once declared:

> Show me the manner in which a nation or community cares for its dead and I will measure with mathematical exactness the tender sympathies of its people, their respect for the law of the land and their loyalty to high ideas.

Ultimately, the choice is yours.

5. The Cost of the Alabaster Box

ONE THING ABOUT THE AMERICAN WAY of death which is a disservice both to the bereaved and to the funeral profession itself is the unjust criticism of the majority of the 65,000 men and women who staff the nation's more than 22,000 funeral homes. This allegedly dismal trade often emerges as the butt of the poor joke, and as the target of self-righteous preachers, self-serving politicians, and self-appointed guardians of public needs and tastes.

To rid the country of these "merchants of mortality," one crusader quite seriously suggested that municipalities have trucks to transport the dead to local crematoria every morning. Although such a program might involve a slight tax hike, it was argued, the public would save between 60 and 70 percent of the amount spent annually on more elaborate rites for their dead.

However, the superficial judgment that a cheap funeral is a good one and an expensive funeral a bad one completely ignores the emotional needs of the persons involved. This is, ultimately, the only important consideration.

Few people have had to avail themselves more of the services of a funeral director than have Joseph Bayly and his wife Mary Lou, a couple who have lost three sons to the tragedy and glory of death. Yet no one has spoken out more forcefully against those who demean the funeral profession than has this nationally known Christian writer.

"We have been told that the funeral director wants maximum profit from his profession," observes Bayly in his book, *The View from a Hearse*. "So do book-writers and medical doctors. My own experience with funeral directors has been quite different from the caricature in the books. I have found them sensitive men in a profession that will probably never be appreciated, because it serves in a context of grief and emotional stress. The funeral director reminds us of death," he adds. "Small wonder that we want to forget him when the hearse is empty."

But not everyone does. In fact, the files of countless funeral directors are stuffed with letters of gratitude from recently bereaved families. This one gives the lie to the so-called high cost of dying and to the allegedly pagan fashions in funerals:

Dear Mr. K____:

How can I thank you for your kindness to me

> and your consideration of our financial stress? But, more than that, the little old lady who shuffled from bed to dresser . . . was gone. Instead, you gave me a woman who appeared thirty years younger—one who seemed ready to open her eyes and talk to us. Our friends kept looking at her and marveled at the transformation. Thanks for everything, Mr. K____, but especially the final memory of my mother as I knew her in healthier, happier years.

If this letter illustrates anything, it is that so many who make light of the restorative arts often have a change of heart when physical deterioration grips the once-strong body of a loved one. Only then many people begin to fully appreciate a profession that provides solace in that final memory of healthier, happier years.

No wonder Joseph Bayly found the funeral director to be "a man with all the feelings and capacities of most human beings," a man who by the nature of his calling "is usually able to help us in our moments of grief, moments when the burdens of decision weigh heaviest."

Nor is it surprising that a well-known Roman Catholic columnist suggested that members of this much-maligned profession have a direct ministry.

> In the early Church there was one honored group that undertook the special office of digging graves, the *fossores,* and to a certain extent our present-day funeral directors have in-

> herited that function. Because of their sensitive relationship with the dead, the bereaved, and the Church, the community expects them to lead lives of sobriety and respectability that almost measure up to those of clerics. They must conduct themselves at least with the gravity and dignity that is expected of the teaching profession, physicians, and lawyers.

So it is not hard to think of the funeral director as a professional. For those who think otherwise, the same writer observes:

> It's no good saying that it's a fairly recent development and recalling the days when the woman next door bathed and dressed the remains and the local furniture dealer supplied the coffin. After all, surgery started in the barbershop. . . .
>
> Undertaking too has a body of relevant information, techniques to be learned, and procedures to be followed. Could you embalm a corpse? Would you know how to get a death certificate? Are you familiar with the burial laws of your state?

It is grossly unfair to condemn a whole profession on the basis of "the shenanigans of a few wildcat operators." To generalize from such outrageous exceptions, is not only mischievous but slanderous.

For Christians and for Jews alike, Joseph E.

McCabe, a United Presbyterian minister, has summed up the heart of the matter regarding these men and women "who sooner or later are called upon to serve every family." He writes in *The Power of God in a Parish Program:* "The funeral director has become indispensable to society, and to many of us a very dear friend. The great majority are men of feeling and honor, and quite often are devoted churchmen. We want his services at the time of sorrow. Therefore, let us express our gratitude to him and pray for him in the comforting ministry to which God has called him."

Not that the funeral profession is above reproach and beyond the scope of reasoned criticism, for funeral directors are no better or any worse than other mortals. But, as Earl Newcomer observes:

> To be sure, there are churchmen and there are some hypocrites.
>
> To be sure, there are bankers and then there are some loan sharks.
>
> To be sure, there are surgeons and then there are quacks.
>
> And, finally, there are funeral directors and then there are "Digger O'Dells."
>
> In every case, the hypocrite is an exception among churchmen; the loan shark is the exception in the banking business; the quack is

> the exception in the surgical profession; and rest assured that the "Digger O'Dell" is the exception in the funeral service profession. We are frank to admit that we do have "Digger O'Dells" in our midst. But, thank God, they are becoming fewer and fewer as they are exposed. Every one of the funeral directors of the United States wants to be judged by the facts—not hearsay. We want to be judged by the true aims and purposes of our profession, and we want every member of the public to know facts about our costs of rendering service. There is nothing that we would intentionally conceal.

What, then, are the facts concerning the so-called high cost of dying? The first fact concerns not so much the funeral director as it does the family in the grip of grief and bereavement. No one will ever be able to assess the emotional havoc caused by "exposes" of American funeral practices. All that can be legitimately said is that purely negative assaults upon the funeral profession can have only a negative effect upon families stricken by death. If people are led to assume that the churches are filled with hypocrites, they will eventually be driven away from the Good News the Church has to proclaim. If people are led to believe that all lawyers are crooked, the entire American judicial system can be fatally undermined. And if people accept the notion that long-treasured funeral practices are a shocking, costly scandal, sooner or later they will lose confidence in a profession that can provide comfort and care in one of the most trying periods of life. One should react prayerfully and critically to any and all attacks upon institutions and traditions which have served the Church and the nation well in the past.

Eternity magazine recently carried a review of a new book, written by one of the most vociferous critics of "the American way of death." The author argues that the prisons are not rehabilitating people, and therefore calls for the abolition of the whole prison system. Although few would debate the weaknesses of American penology, few would advocate such radical corrective action!

This same author in an earlier book concluded that the real sting of death awaits survivors who pay the bills. Moreover, it was alleged, the real victory over the grave "has been won hands down by a funeral establishment—in disastrously unequal battle."

It must be admitted that some families go completely overboard in making their funeral arrangements—some to make amends, some to diminish guilt, some to keep up with the Joneses. However, as Joseph Bayly points out, "A funeral can be as simple and inexpensive as the law allows and the decision-maker desires. If caskets have become more ornate and expensive, if cemeteries have become more country-club-like, if services provided by the funeral director have become increasingly elaborate, it is because we have demanded these things." The funeral director himself is merely the executor of the family's wishes and guided by the laws of the city and state.

A closely related second fact involves the role of rite and ceremony in what Elton Trueblood has termed "the common ventures of life." As Christians, ceremony accompanies our baptisms, the confirmation of those vows, and the covenant of holy matrimony. Why should it seem strange then that, when life ends, we should dignify our dead with a ceremony that, in our culture, has become not only a rite for the dead, but a right of the living?

"A funeral without the body present," says C. M. Franklin, "is like a baptism without the baby, a wedding without the bride and the bridegroom, and a birthday without the birthday child." For this reason many experts on death and grief strenuously object to the immediate disposition of the body, with a memorial service some time later.

"The funeral service is psychologically necessary in order to give the opportunity for 'grief work,' " says psychiatrist Eric Lindemann. "The bereaved must be given the capacity to work through his grief if he is to come out of that situation emotionally sound."

Another psychiatrist, James A. Knight, agrees. In a normal grief reaction, he says, "the work of mourning must be done, the bondage to the deceased broken, and new relationships formed. The rituals and customs associated with death and dying should be understood and evaluated from the standpoint of how well they help people do the necessary work of mourning and how well they succeed in preventing pathological grief reactions which now or later lead to illness."

Meanwhile, Dr. Andrew Watson, a Michigan psychiatrist, attributes much of the blame for grief pathology to the manner in which so many people die in contemporary society. "A loved one dies behind curtains in a hospital room," he notes. "His body is quickly cremated, or his coffin is shut. There is no closing of the relationship, no opportunity to say good-bye, no way in which we can feel the death that we rationally know has come."

According to Dr. Henry Grunebaum of the Massachusetts Health Center, even the woman who delivers a stillborn child needs the opportunity to vent her grief. Dr. Grunebaum cites the case of an expectant mother who "was helpless during the delivery, not allowed to see the baby, and encouraged to sign an autopsy and burial permit for a mass grave. We may wonder whether her grieving would not have proceeded more normally," he says, "had she seen her baby and been able to give it an appropriate funeral service."

Traditional funeral rites can actually offer the bereaved not only a rational means to express grief but also a deep and abiding sense of relief. Dr. Charles W. Wahl, chief of UCLA's Psychosomatic Service, tells of a friend whose mother died from a chronic and wasting illness. "At the funeral service," he says, "my friend experienced a deep and profound consolation seeing his mother with the lines of suffering erased from her face and lying in peace."

Of equal importance, the funeral service provides what Dr. William M. Lamers, Jr., has called "an organized, purposeful, time limited, flexible, group-centered response to death." What this West Coast psychiatrist is saying may have first been articulated by St. Augustine 1,500 years ago. On the one hand, Augustine stressed that "it is a natural duty that we pay respect to the body," since it was "the organ and instrument used by the soul in the performance of good works." On the other hand, he added, "the burial rites . . . are more of a consolation to the living than of assistance to the dead."

That St. Augustine was an expert on the psychology of grief is indicated by a story told by a Wisconsin funeral director who had been called by a young woman to arrange for her mother's immediate cremation. Since state law did not permit immediate disposal in such cases, the director suggested that he call the woman's minister to arrange for private services. "Don't list the funeral as private," she exclaimed. "Nobody will come anyway."

In subsequent counseling, the director learned that this woman had never attended a funeral and that her initial desires were based on the fact that her mother looked so terrible at the hospital. With the restorative arts, however, the agony and horror picture of death was removed, giving the bereaved young woman a genuine feeling of consolation.

"She changed her mind about cremation," the director later wrote, "and now wanted her mother buried next to her father in a cemetery in northern Wisconsin. Incidentally, the funeral home was filled to capacity that afternoon, filled with friends who had put aside their work that day just to share with the daughter a moment of respect and dignity for a human life now ended."

No wonder that Paul E. Irion, a noted pastoral psychologist, has said: "The funeral can be an experience of value as it meets the needs of those who mourn." Indeed, it was the recognition of this fact that led a church in Minneapolis to establish a Healing Fellowship for those who have experienced bereavement. As one participant put it: "One of the finest healing agents for the sorrowful heart is the healing fellowship of Christian friends."

It is for this reason that both Protestants and Roman Catholics have conceived of death as a corporate event in the fellowship of believers. "The impact of death is realized and experienced in the community of faith," says Merle R. Jordan, another noted pastoral psychologist. "And it calls forth the caring resources of the congregation to the bereaved."

The American Lutheran Church has published a booklet, *Appointed Once to Die,* which defines the funeral as "a public expression of Christian solidarity when death comes to a member of the Christian community."

The booklet declares, "Every such symbol of Christian solidarity gives opportunity to friends and relatives of the deceased to share in the supporting warmth and strength of Christian fellowship." Moreover, it adds, traditional funeral rites provide the opportunity to present "the living way of salvation found only in Jesus Christ, and offer a public confession of victorious, triumphant faith."

"Little meaning would there be to the Christian burial service," says the Rev. Roderick D. Sheldon, "if the resurrection of Jesus Christ were not a proven fact. This truth, and His promise of coming again, when He shall call unto Himself from the graves all those who 'love His appearing,' make the Christian burial service a sacred privilege, a solemn memorial, and a loving expression of an assured expectation."

When Christians gather before the casket of a fellow believer, they not only witness to their own faith in the resurrection, but they also witness against the blind unbelief of the ages—whether that unbelief be exhibited in the paganism of the ancient past, or in a modern paganism which can send off a propped-up corpse holding a martini glass in a lifeless hand!

The Bible itself is replete with illustrations of the burial practices of the saints. Take the story of Abraham, who left the comforts of Ur of the Chaldees to strike out "for a city which hath foundations, whose builder and maker is God" (Heb. 11:10). With him on his life's pilgrimage went his wife, Sarah, who died before him in the land of promise. "And after this," it says in the Bible, "Abraham buried Sarah his wife in the cave of the field of Machpelah . . . and the field, and the cave that is therein, were made sure unto Abraham for a possession of a burying-place" (Gen. 23:19,20).

Although archaeologists have determined that Abraham paid his pagan neighbors far more than the market value of the land, he had no complaints about the high cost of dying for he was paying a final, loving tribute to his wife. Also, he was witnessing to his faith that the God of the promises keeps His covenant in death, no less than in life. "Wherefore," says the Bible, "God is not ashamed to be called their God: for he hath prepared for them a city" (Heb. 11:16).

However, the story of the impending death of our Lord should be even more instructive for Christians who are tempted to repress all emotion and permit purely utilitarian considerations to guide their thoughts on traditional funeral practices. As the end drew near, Mary took a pound of costly spikenard, anointed the feet of her Master, and then wiped His feet with her hair. It was her way of witnessing before all those assembled that in life or in death she was absolutely committed to Jesus Christ. But Judas took an entirely different view of the matter. "Why was not this ointment sold for three hundred denarii," he asked, "and given to the poor?"

"To him the woman's offering was mere sentiment and waste," observes the Reverend Ronald D. Harmer. "Judas measured life by the wrong standard; he could see this alabaster box and its contents only in the light of utilitarian and material value." Judas really did not care about the poor. Similarly, one might ponder the real motives of those who would abandon rite and tradition during bereavement.

Thank God for Jesus Christ. "Jesus knew Mary's heart and her motive," says Dr. Harmer. "She did not do it for show or display. She did it because in her heart of hearts she looked about for some special way of expressing her feeling, and this was the way she found."

Far from supporting the crusading Judas, Jesus accepted the love and affection in the spirit it was offered. "Let her alone," He declared. "Against the day of my burying, hath she kept this" (Jn. 12:7). Those who think that Jesus was merely accommodating Himself to the neurotic impulses of an emotional and high-strung woman should think again. Matthew records:

> When it was evening, there came a rich man from Arimathea, named Joseph, who also was a disciple of Jesus. He went to Pilate and asked for the body of Jesus. Then Pilate ordered it to be given to him. And Joseph took the body, and wrapped it in a clean linen shroud, and laid it in his own new tomb, which he had hewn in the rock; and he rolled a great stone to the door of the tomb, and departed (Mt. 27:57-60, RSV).

Moreover, says Luke, the women who followed Jesus from Galilee went to the sepulcher themselves to make certain that all was in order. "And they returned," he adds, "and prepared spices and ointments; and rested the sabbath day according to the commandment" (Lk. 23:56).

Those who loved the Master in life did not wait and hold a memorial service weeks after His death. "Instead," says the Reverend M. Dudley Rose, "the physical remains were treated with reverence and respect."

Therefore, Christians should think twice about proposals that would discard a human body as if it were a broken toy. "At the time of death," said John Wesley, "we need to pay proper respect to what was once a temple of the Holy Spirit."

The same sentiment has been expressed by the Reverend Vernon O. Elmore, who has traced contempt for the body back to Greek paganism. "The person has been identified with the body so intimately that family and friends can scarcely dissociate the two," he says. "To honor the body is to honor the person. . . .

"I thank God for Joseph of Arimathea and Nicodemus who felt it a religious duty to see to the proper burial of Jesus. I have a warm spot in my heart for the woman who came early to the tomb with spices to anoint His body. It is altogether appropriate for Christians today to lovingly and respectfully prepare the body for burial and to accord it funeral honors."

Those who pay a final, loving tribute to a friend or loved one also are helping themselves to adjust to the tragedy and triumph of death. As a well-known authority on grief so aptly put it:

> A funeral faces the reality of death. It does not avoid it.
>
> A funeral provides a setting wherein the religious needs of the bereaved may be satisfied.

A funeral provides faith to sustain spirit.

A funeral helps to free one from guilt and self-condemnation.

A funeral helps one to express feelings.

A funeral directs one beyond the death of a loved one to face life's ongoing responsibilities unafraid.

A funeral, in a personal way, helps one face a crisis with courage and dignity.

A funeral provides an environment in which loving friends and relatives can give strength to those who are bereaved.

Above all, the Christian funeral helps the living to number their days (Ps. 90:12), even as it directs the uncommitted to turn their lives and wills over to the care of a gracious God who has loved His own even unto death itself.

It has therefore been rightly observed that contempt or respect for the body actually reflects a culture's philosophy as to man's innate worth and dignity. This is indicated by a well-known story concerning the Russian revolutionary, V. I. Lenin, who became so wrapped up in radical enterprise that he lost the capacity for human compassion and tenderness. Lenin's wife, Krupskaya, had been keeping a 24-hour watch over her dying mother. Finally, exhausted, she begged her husband to look after her mother while she tried to get a little rest. Lenin reportedly agreed.

However, Krupskaya awakened the next morning to find her husband still writing another revolutionary tract—and her mother dead. Angered and distraught, she confronted the famous radical with his broken promise. But he coldly replied: "You told me to awaken you if your mother needed you. She died. She didn't need you."

Lenin's estimate of the value of human life has been amply documented by writers and historians such as Solzhenitsyn. Lest we conclude, however, that only certain societies are prone to such attitudes, we need to remember that the average Hollywood Western shows much the same callous disregard for the dead.

In a word, respect for the dead is an accurate indicator of the value placed upon the living.

6. Not As a Stranger

THE TELEPHONE SEEMED TO BEAR only the news of tragedy that sunny autumn morning.

First there was a call from a church member who said her husband of half a century was on the "critical list" after undergoing hemodialysis for kidney failure for three agonizing years.

Then came a call from a friend at the funeral home, inquiring whether I could minister to the family of a man who died at 27 of lingering cancer.

The morning mail was no more cheerful, for it contained a letter informing me that an auto accident had killed a brilliant young woman who recently received her Ph.D.

As I reflected upon all this, the thought kept recurring that, in spite of all the euphemisms, there never can be any dignity in death. Rather, the extinction of life is its final indignity. Indeed, the

Scriptures declare that death is the last enemy to be destroyed (I Cor. 15:26).

When death strikes, it may claim a child slaughtered by a deranged parent, a teenager killed on a motorcycle, a mother's son on the field of battle, a business executive in the prime of life, or a rugged individualist wasting away from disease.

Death may wear many masks. But all inspire a sense of the tragic and deep feelings of revulsion. Yet the conspiracy of silence with which we so often surround dying led the British anthropologist Geoffrey Gorer to coin the phrase "the pornography of death."

"In the 19th Century the great unmentionable subject was sex," observes the Reverend Winfield S. Haycock. "In this century the great unmentionable word is death. In both practice and theory we persistently hide death from the living. In our dreams we pretend that medical science, which has lengthened our lives by some years, will soon have done away with death completely."

It is ironical that among those most interested in the new science of cryonics are those who deny the possibility of Christian life after death. Although they refuse to take that leap of faith into God's arms, they express no such lack of daring when it comes to having their bodies scientifically frozen at the point of death in the hope of some future resuscitation. Jesus said:

> Lay not up for yourselves treasures upon earth, where moth and rust doth corrupt, and

> where thieves break through and steal: but lay up for yourselves treasures in heaven, where neither moth nor rust doth corrupt, and where thieves do not break through nor steal: for where your treasure is, there will your heart be also (Mt. 6:19-21).

This wisdom is especially pertinent in an age in which science has become the sacred cow. In his blindness, ancient man bowed before the totems of his clans, while his modern counterpart, in his presumed enlightenment, bows before the altar of an admittedly more exact alchemy.

Science already has accomplished what was seemingly unthinkable in years past: breaking the genetic code, producing forms of life in a test tube, eradicating diseases which once crippled and killed men like flies.

But science also has produced a technology that may threaten our lives. It can either trigger a holocaust or bend the minds of men themselves into predictable and socially acceptable behavioral patterns.

The natural sciences have not been alone in wrenching man from his once-sturdy religious moorings. Classical Freudians have told him that his spiritual strivings are but a form of mass neurosis, while Marxists insist that sermons on immortality are opiates or narcotics for dulling the senses to pain.

Such supposed advancements led Franklin H. Littell of Temple University to plead for a renewed balance between science and wisdom. "It is one of the ironies of this self-styled 'scientific' age," he says, "that it has produced more new myths and rituals than a fat notebook can record." These have left their imprint upon modern man's mind. He tends to be more earthbound and materialistic than his forebears, for he has been assured that he now resides in the post-Christian era.

Oddly enough, however, the age in which God is defied and death denied also has been characterized as the "Age of Anxiety." Instead of liberating man from his fears and phobias, the modern mood has compounded his existential problem. Individuals are now painfully aware that it is not easy to become the captain of one's soul and the master of one's fate. Indeed, the new prophet of doom is often the thorough-going secularist who shudders to think that the Age of Aquarius might well usher in the Age of the Apocalypse.

It was against just this sort of pervasive pessimism that the Christian doctrines of the nature and destiny of man were forged. Their object is not only to offer men hope in the hereafter but strength for the here and now. When the Bible comments upon the burning issues of life and death, it does so with refreshing realism and candor. As Paul Tournier observes:

> The Bible does not minimize the importance of death, like the Stoics of antiquity or the Orientals of our own day. It takes death seriously; it describes with heart-rending realism

the anguish that men experience in the presence of death, and the overwhelming catastrophe of it. It does indeed bring us the triumphal shout of faith, like that of St. Paul: "For to me to live is Christ, and to die is gain" (Philippians 1:21). But even the most lively faith does not spare man the anxiety of death.

I. *The Christian faith, then, does not ignore man's natural fear of death.* Rather, it agrees with Samuel Johnson that "no rational man can face death without uneasy apprehension." But it also shares John Bunyan's vision of Christian and Hopeful crossing the river of death on their way to the gate of the eternal city:

> The pilgrims then began to inquire if there was no other way to the gate; to which (two men in raiment that shone like gold) answered, Yes; but there hath not any, save two, to wit, Enoch and Elijah, been permitted to tread that path, since the foundation of the world, nor shall, until the last trumpet shall sound. The pilgrims then, especially Christian, began to despond in their minds, and looked this way and that, but no way could be found by them, by which they might escape the river. Then they asked the men if the waters were all of a depth. They said, No; yet they could not help them in that case; for, said they, you shall find it deeper or shallower, as you believe in the King of the place.

> They then addressed themselves to the water; and entering, Christian began to sink, and crying out to his good friend Hopeful, he said, I sink in deep waters; the billows go over my head, all his waves go over me! Selah.

> Then said the other, Be of good cheer, my brother, I feel the bottom, and it is good.

Unfortunately, Christian was overwhelmed by the fear that he would never "see the land that flows with milk and honey." His anxiety increased as he reflected upon "the sins that he had committed, both since and before he began to be a pilgrim."

Yet Hopeful was reassuring:

> These troubles and distresses that you go through in these waters are no sign that God hath forsaken you, but are sent to try you, whether you will call to mind that which heretofore you have received of His goodness, and live upon Him in your distresses.

Finally, both Christian and Hopeful crossed the river safely and appeared before the King's gate. And, as they entered, "they were transfigured, and they had raiment put on that shone like gold."

Unhappily, the skeptic tends to get bogged down with the symbolism, thereby missing the more essential elements of the allegory. It is not so much a matter of Heaven being up there or out there, but rather a question of man's own anxieties regarding his moral condition and fear of the unknown.

To those who facetiously say they do not want to spend eternity playing harps, C. S. Lewis replies that Biblical imagery is merely a "symbolic attempt to express the inexpressible." He writes:

> Musical instruments are mentioned because for many people (not all) music is the thing known in the present life which most strongly suggests ecstasy and infinity. Crowns are mentioned to suggest the fact that those who are united with God in eternity share His splendor and power and joy. Gold is mentioned to suggest the timelessness of heaven (gold does not rust) and the preciousness of it. People who take these symbols literally might as well think that when Christ told us to be like doves, He meant that we were to lay eggs.

Lewis hints that man's skepticism springs not so much from intellectual doubt as from moral culpability. "We have cause," he says, "to be uneasy. There is nothing indulgent about the moral law. It is as hard as nails. It tells you to do the straight thing and it does not seem to care how painful, or dangerous, or difficult it is to do."

If there is just an impersonal power behind this law, he argues, there is no sense in requesting that allowances be made for you, "just as there is no sense in asking the multiplication table to let you off when you do your sums wrong.'' In both cases, he suggests, ''you are bound to get the wrong answer.''

But that is not all. ''If the universe is not governed by an absolute goodness,'' he insists, ''then all our efforts are in the long run hopeless. But if it is, then we are making ourselves enemies to that goodness every day, and are not in the least likely to do any better tomorrow, and so our case is hopeless again. We cannot do without it, and we cannot do with it.'' From the Christian perspective, he concludes:

> God is the only comfort, He is also the supreme terror: the thing we must need and the thing we most want to hide from. He is our only possible ally, and we have made ourselves His enemies.
>
> Some people talk as if meeting the gaze of absolute goodness would be fun. They need to think again. They are still only playing with religion. Goodness is either the great safety or the great danger—according to the way you react to it. And we have reacted the wrong way.

However, a knowledge of moral culpability represents only one side of the coin. The other is a natural fear of the unknown, shared by even some of the staunchest saints.

A Scottish doctor one day visited a dying patient.

As he sat by the bedside, the old man asked if he knew what he could expect "beyond the door." Although momentarily perplexed, the doctor heard his dog scratching outside the room.

"Do you hear that scratching at the door?" he asked. "That is my dog. Although the door is shut, he hears my voice and wants to come in. Now is that not the same with you? We do not know exactly what lies beyond the door, but we do know that our Master awaits us there."

That is the most honest Christian answer to the universal fear of death. But overshadowing that fear is the Gospel promise: "Eye hath not seen, nor ear heard, neither have entered into the heart of man, the things which God hath prepared for them that love him" (I Cor. 2:9). And the believer's response is:

> The Lord is my shepherd; I shall not want . . . Yea, though I walk through the valley of the shadow of death, I will fear no evil: for thou art with me; . . . and I will dwell in the house of the Lord for ever (Ps. 23).

II. *The Christian faith also deals squarely with the tragedy of death itself.* "The modern fashion is to call death by euphemisms—a passing away, a calm after life's fitful fever, a glorious adventure, or whatever one's fancy prefers," observes the Reverend Carroll E. Simcox. "But instinctively we feel that death is tragic; and Christianity corroborates our instinct."

Dr. Simcox, editor of *The Living Church,* notes that our first reaction is to mourn the loss of a loved one. "The reaction is right," he says. "When death takes away from us the life of a valued person, we and our present world are the losers." He writes:

> If this is the way you react to bereavement, and if you wonder if this is a betrayal of your Christian faith, put your mind at rest: your reaction is Christian and right. The shortest text in the Bible reads simply, "Jesus wept" (John 11:35). It is instinctive. Jesus was weeping at the grave of His friend Lazarus. His weeping was His recognition of the tragic nature of death. Lazarus may well be better off, in a better world, in consequence of his death; but his devoted sisters and his friends are heartbroken in this world because he is gone from it. This is death's tragedy: that it takes from our world precious lives which our world cannot afford to lose.

Death is no less tragic for the person who himself must soon die, for there is often the feeling that there is still so much love to give, so much more to learn, so many more things to do.

One thought dominated the mind of that 27-year-old husband and father dying of cancer. He would never have the quiet joy of watching his two-year-old daughter develop into a mature young woman.

Consequently, many Christians experience that

universal flush of anger when they first look into death's mocking face. Dr. Paul Tournier recalls a committed Christian woman patient who died in the prime of life. Before her death, she confided to him: "When I realized . . . that death was not far off, I felt shattered and rebellious. I cried out inside of myself: No, I won't die. It isn't fair at my age. . . . At the same time I was reproaching myself for these interior explosions: a Christian woman such as I ought to be accepting death quite differently. But it was too strong for me. I was kicking against death with everything I had."

Dr. Tournier explained that the Bible was an infinitely human book. "It understands and shares," he said, "the natural horror of life faced with death, and does not condemn it." He then reminded her that the Bible calls death "the king of terrors" (Job 18:14) and an enemy so great that it will be the last to be defeated (I Cor. 15:26). Even Jesus, faced with the ignominy of the Cross, cried out: "My God, my God, why hast thou forsaken me?" (Mt. 27:46).

"We had a long talk together about death," says Dr. Tournier, "and about the realism of the Bible, which brings us the certainties of faith, but does not therefore claim to take away from us the awful pangs through which we must pass. Fear of death is not lack of faith. To keep one's faith is not to be superhuman, to imagine that one is not subject to fear; it means rather admitting one's natural rebelliousness and confessing it, and receiving, thereafter, supernatural strength to overcome it."

III. *The Christian faith offers an explanation as to death's origin.* Although its answer may not dissuade the confirmed skeptic, it does help many who ask in their bereavement: How can anyone believe in God in a world like this?

This question is almost as old as man himself. Job pondered on the meaning of life and death as he faced unrelieved and seemingly unwarranted torment. His wife's counsel was to curse God and die. From the human perspective, this response would have been quite understandable. The Bible itself declares that Job was "perfect and upright, and one that feared God, and eschewed evil" (Job 1:1). Yet he lost virtually all that he possessed, even his children, while he suffered pain and disease. In his torment, Job raised all of the questions asked by those who have witnessed war's horrors, the pain on the face of a loved one, or the open grave of a small child.

However, it was during this experience that he said:

> I know that my redeemer liveth, and that he shall stand at the latter day upon the earth: and though after my skin worms destroy this body, yet in my flesh shall I see God (Job 19:25,26).

The Bible makes it indelibly clear that God created a perfect world free of sin, and sickness, disease, and death. The only sanction imposed upon Adam and Eve was not to eat of the tree of the knowledge of good and evil. "For in the day that thou eatest thereof," said the Lord, "thou shalt surely die" (Gen. 2:17).

Then Satan came in to destroy this balance in nature. "Ye shall not surely die," he claimed. "For God doth know that in the day that ye eat thereof, then your eyes shall be opened, and ye shall be as gods, knowing good and evil" (Gen. 3:4,5).

Although many dismiss this Biblical narrative as mere fantasy, it is filled with profound and abiding truths. Adam and Eve *did* eat of the forbidden fruit, and we, their children, continue to make the willful decision to play God and to conduct our lives on our own terms. However, as Pascal wrote: "In seeking to become angels, we may become less than men."

God's prohibition was not based upon a capricious divine will, but upon a loving desire to protect man from himself and to assure creation's order of perfection. By disobeying, man was not only alienated from God but cut off from the Source of life itself. For, as Jacques Ellul suggests, the divine sanction was more a warning than a threat. It was like advising mankind that it is dangerous to touch high-tension wires. The inevitable result is death.

Apart from man's spiritual death, Dr. Tournier contends that physical and social suffering were involved in the divine sanction. These are symbolized, he says, "by the pains of childbirth and the difficulty man will have in winning his bread" (see Gen. 3:17-19). "The two aspects of death are inseparable," he says. "Spiritual death, entering into man, will be manifested sooner or later in his physiological death." He illustrates this from experiments in the artificial culture of living tissues:

> Previously, it had been thought that, from the scientific point of view, we should die because we are made of organic tissues that were destined to die, that it was the death of the parts that brought about the death of the organism as a whole. Such is by no means the case, since these parts, suitably cultivated, can continue to live indefinitely beyond the time that they would have died if left in the organism. It is therefore the destiny of the organism as a whole that governs the death of the parts.

"In Christian doctrine," writes Professor Jacques Courvoisier, "death . . . does not figure as the end of a normal process, but as the result of a state of things disordered from the beginning." However, he says, God mercifully delays the natural outcome of man's disobedience by coming to his aid. He helps to retard death—to prolong this respite of debt—during which a man may turn to Jesus Christ and, through faith in Him, find forgiveness, and victory over death through the resurrection.

IV. *Finally, the Christian faith offers the promise of death's defeat.* The Bible itself expresses this hope:

> For as in Adam all die, even so in Christ shall

> all be made alive. But every man in his own order: Christ the first fruits; afterward they that are Christ's at his coming. Then cometh the end, when he shall have delivered up the kingdom to God, even the Father; when he shall have put down all rule and all authority and power. For he must reign, till he hath put all enemies under his feet. The last enemy that shall be destroyed is death (I Cor. 15:22-26).

What are the alternatives to this Christian conviction regarding death's ultimate defeat?

First is the notion that death demands an adventurous step into the unknown. As the great philosopher Socrates took the hemlock, he told his friends: "The hour of departure has arrived, and we go our ways—I to die, and you to live. Which is better, God only knows."

Another pagan view of death suggests that death will come easier if we despise life. In *Macbeth,* Malcolm expresses this idea as he reports Cawdor's execution:

> Nothing in his life
> Became him like the leaving it; he died
> As one that hath been studied in his death
> To throw away the dearest thing he owned
> As 'twere a careless trifle.

Closely related is the idea that death involves the personality's total extinction, a descent into nothingness. "This view of death can be comforting," observes Carroll Simcox. "If life has been a horror or a hell for one, death as a simple ceasing-to-be may appear as a very sweet blessing."

However, the problem with all these views is that they are pagan. Unlike Socrates, the Christian can say with the apostle Paul: "For to me to live is Christ, and to die is gain" (Phil. 1:21). Moreover, he should never despise life, because to do so is to despise its Giver. He will not call life a curse since, as Dr. Simcox suggests, that "is to call God a fiend for inflicting it."

With the monumental strides being made in medical science, the pessimism of earlier paganism is being replaced by a paganism of naive optimism, which dismisses out of hand the reasoned discourse of thoughtful Christian scholars such as Ellul, Courvoisier, and Tournier.

Philosopher F. M. Esfandiary recently said in *The New York Times* that, thanks to science, it will "soon be possible to extend human life indefinitely." He wrote:

> Death is the cruelest indignity. There is dignity only in living. If dying is *natural,* then the hell with the tyranny of nature. Why be resigned to it? Let us continue to rise above nature. Who are those urging us to accept death? They are individuals programmed by the Puritan old world of guilt and punishment to regard suffering and death as necessities. In desperation they hold on to fantasies of life after death.

Calling for "a new philosophy of life free of guilt and resignation," Esfandiary sees "the upheaval against aging and death" advancing in two stages:

> Stage one involves stop-gap measures to prolong life: Drugs to help reverse cell-blockage that leads to cell-death and aging. Estrogen pills, anti-oxydents, and anti-aging drugs. Control of diet particularly by reducing calorie intake (meats and dairy products).
>
> Also, revitalizing of the immunity systems of the elderly to help them combat diseases. Lowering of the body temperature by a couple of degrees. Biofeedback training for better control of brain waves and body functions. Transplants.
>
> Anabiosis, or freezing of the body immediately after death until a suitable time in the future when the body can be revived.
>
> Stage two is a longer-range effort not simply to forestall death but to overcome it altogether.
>
> This includes extensive genetic modifications in the human body, introducing self-regulating parts to enable us to live indefinitely and adapt to new habitats in space.
>
> Then, too, we will refine the existing ability to replace more and more of our vulnerable body

> parts. We will continue to de-animalize our bodies, creating new durable attractive physiologies.

In an age when man can travel into interstellar space and decode light from the presumed edges of the universe, says Esfandiary, "it is outrageous that such a beautiful phenomenon as intelligent, sentient life should be encased in such fleeting vulnerable bodies." He concludes that it is time to "marshal our genius to achieve the most transcendent and liberating freedom of all—physical immortality."

Far be it from Christian scholarship to deny the staggering advances in science and technology. However, Esfandiary's vision of a world victorious over physical mortality raises several pertinent problems:

1. It may tackle the weakness of man's physical frame; but it says nothing about man's moral nature. Would it therefore really be a blessing to reside eternally in a world still beset by man's inhumanity to man?
2. It bequeaths upon the scientist, himself a mortal, the characteristics of omnipotence.
3. It also offers little hope for the individual who weeps over the open grave of a loved one NOW! In fact, for such people, its only message is one of despair, since life after death is perceived as a mere vestige of a crude and obsolete Christian heritage.
4. Finally, it involves a leap of faith of its

own—a leap of faith predicated, not upon the existence of an all-powerful and beneficent Deity, but rather upon frail, fumbling, and faltering man himself.

Those attracted to the vision of man as his own salvation might like to ponder the words of the Reverend Robert P. Montgomery, Presbyterian chaplain at Princeton University. Speaking on "The Power of Positive Suffering," he related that John heard a voice speaking to him like a trumpet "on his non-psychedelic trip" to Heaven. "Come up here," the voice declared, "and I will show you what must happen hereafter" (Rev. 4:1, NEB). Then Dr. Montgomery continued:

> This insight into the future was to be found in the scroll that he saw in God's hand, but it was sealed with seven seals and there was no one worthy in heaven or earth to open it. John wept bitter tears, he tells us, "because no one was found worthy to open the scroll"—and hence to forecast the future.
>
> Not that there weren't plenty of volunteers:
>
> "Look—I'm Phi Beta Kappa—prepped at Groton, undergraduate at Princeton, Ph.D. from Harvard—who could be more worthy?
>
> I can understand why those eggheads don't qualify, but me—I'm a hardheaded, down-to-

earth businessman—the president of a large corporation—surely I'm worthy. . . ."

"But are you worthy?" asked Dr. Montgomery, when hell itself is the haven of all such arrogance, including that more subtle arrogance of humility about which Nietzsche spoke, illustrated so well in the woman about whom it was said, "She lived for others; you could recognize the others by their hunted look."

If not before by the grace of God, Dr. Montgomery declared, all men will resolve their much-discussed identity crisis in the face of death. "There we will desert our fantasy worlds," he observed. "There we will not recite how we published rather than perished. . . . There we will not want to recite what a killing we made on the market. There we will know who we are: 'God be merciful to me a sinner.' "

Like it or not, that cry of submission before the divine Sovereign opens the gates of Heaven. "Behold, I stand at the door, and knock," says Christ. "If any man hear my voice, and open the door, I will come in to him, and will sup with him, and he with me" (Rev. 3:20).

In a word, we can go out into eternity to meet Jesus Christ either as a stranger or as a friend.

What is involved in this divine promise is no mere pie in the sky in the sweet bye and bye. Rather, it represents a pledge which offers daily support in the hard-pressed here and now.

This fact has been brought home to me time and

again as I have conducted scores of funeral services, both for committed Christians and for those of little or no faith. In the latter category, there was the beautiful young woman who died of a drug overdose, the TV executive deep into Oriental mysticism, the 87-year-old wealthy spinster who attended a cocktail party the night before her death, and numerous others who died "having a form of godliness, but denying the power thereof" (II Tim. 3:5).

The officiating clergyman often can sense the chill which marks the funeral rites of such people. Sometimes the inner despair is masked by an alcoholic fog. On other occasions, the mourners begin arguing about the division of the estate even before the committal services. But most often there is a blank or uneasy look when God's Word is proclaimed.

In such instances, the clergyman is faced with one of three alternatives: to offer no hope whatever, to overtly evangelize, or to simply proclaim the Gospel.

The temptation to offer no hope can entrap some in the sin of spiritual pride. For the Scriptures declare: "The Lord seeth not as man seeth; for man looketh on the outward appearance, but the Lord looketh on the heart" (I Sam. 16:7). Moreover, Abraham asks, "Shall not the Judge of all the earth do right?" (Gen. 18:25).

The significance of such passages was indelibly impressed upon me in the case of that young narcotics victim. At one point she had found release after turning to Jesus Christ, only to be ensnared again in bondage. However, the Judge of all may someday turn to her Christian friends and ask them what *they* did to protect her from the downward spiral of addiction.

A thin line exists between tactless evangelism and "holding forth the word of life" (Phil. 2:16). Evangelicals might well learn a lesson from the new Roman Catholic funeral liturgy, which is thoroughly Biblical, universal in its appeal, and challenging.

On few other occasions do pastors have the opportunity to witness to hearts suddenly opened to the Gospel's claims and to human frailty. An open casket is sometimes worth a thousand sermons, so the service is a time to be used prayerfully, wisely, and lovingly.

I have often used an illustration from the life of Cecil B. De Mille, a devout Christian and well-known motion-picture producer. While out in a canoe he noticed a large black beetle which was slowly dying. However, De Mille suddenly realized that its outer shell was beginning to crack open. Then, almost imperceptibly, he could see taking shape the beautiful wings of a butterfly, which then soared over the water.

"The thought occurred to me," he wrote, "that I had witnessed a miracle—a metamorphosis. For out of the mud and slime had come a beautiful new life. And I thought silently, if God could do this to one of the least of His creatures, what does He have in store for the human spirit?"

Christians believe there's an even greater change

awaiting them in Christ Jesus. Our confession of faith is not restricted to the soul's immortality but extends to the body's resurrection. Of course it won't be a body still subject to sickness, suffering, aches, and pains. The Apostle Paul says:

> Now this I say, brethren, that flesh and blood cannot inherit the kingdom of God; neither doth corruption inherit incorruption. For this corruptible must put on incorruption. . . . So when . . . this mortal shall have put on immortality, then shall be brought to pass the saying that is written, Death is swallowed up in victory. O death, where is thy sting? O grave, where is thy victory? (I Cor. 15:50, 53-55).

With this conviction the apostolic church diverged from a prevailing ancient Greek notion of the soul's amorphous immortality. Rather, the early Christians were steadfast in their belief that our personalities will survive the grave and that we will know even as also we are known (I Cor. 13:12).

Saints through the centuries have not abandoned this hope. "Some day you will read in the newspapers that D. L. Moody is dead," the great evangelist on one occasion remarked. "But don't believe a word of it. For in that instant I shall be more alive than I am now."

What a difference when a pastor conducts the funeral service of a Christian. Of course his loved ones share that universal sense of the tragedy and agony of separation, but they know it is only temporary. And the comforting words of Scripture take on added weight for them:

> Our help is in the name of the Lord, who made heaven and earth (Ps. 124:8).
>
> The eternal God is thy refuge, and underneath are the everlasting arms (Deut. 33:27).
>
> Like as a father pitieth his children, so the Lord pitieth them that fear him (Ps. 103:13).
>
> As one whom his mother comforteth, so will I comfort you; and ye shall be comforted (Isa. 66:13).
>
> Peace I leave with you, my peace I give unto you: not as the world giveth, give I unto you. Let not your heart be troubled, neither let it be afraid (Jn. 14:27).
>
> God is our refuge and strength, a very present help in trouble. Therefore will not we fear (Ps. 46:1, 2).
>
> Jesus said . . . I am the resurrection, and the life: he that believeth in me, though he were dead, yet shall he live: and whosoever liveth and believeth in me shall never die (Jn. 11:25, 26).

For those who have had true communion with

Christ in life, most pastors prefer to have the services in the church, the spiritual home of the deceased. During the service, the casket is generally closed so that all eyes are directed to the living Christ. Often the casket is draped with a funeral pall to symbolize the equality of all men before their Maker.

And then the minister commits his fellow believer "to the ground, earth to earth, ashes to ashes, dust to dust, in the sure and certain hope of the resurrection to eternal life; through Jesus Christ our Lord."

Merely the pious words of professional Christians? Not on your life!

When Dr. W. E. Sangster, England's great Methodist preacher, lay dying with muscular atrophy, he wrote to his friend Dr. Billy Graham: "All my life I have preached that Jesus Christ is adequate for every crisis. I have but a few days to live, and oh, Billy, Christ is indeed adequate in the hour of death. Tell everyone it is true."

A similar shout of victory came from Dr. Clarence MaCartney, long-time pastor of Pittsburgh's First Presbyterian Church. As he lay dying, his last message to his congregation was: "Tell them the Anchor still holds!"*

That is what Christian faith is all about: to enter eternity to meet Jesus Christ, not as a stranger, but as a Friend!

*Hebrews 6:19: "Which hope we have as an anchor of the soul, both sure and stedfast. . . ."

APPENDIX 1

UNIFORM DONOR CARD

OF ______________________________

Print or Type name of donor

In the hope that I may help others, I hereby make this anatomical gift, if medically acceptable, to take effect upon my death. The words and marks below indicate my desires.

I give: (a)______any needed organs or parts
(b)______only the following organs or parts:

____

Specify the organ(s) or part(s)

for the purposes of transplantation, therapy, medical research or education.

(c)______my body for anatomical study if needed.

Limitations or
special wishes, if any: ______________________

Signed by the donor and the following two witnesses in the presence of each other:

____

Signature of Donor Date of Birth

____

Date Signed City & State

____

Witness Witness

This is a legal document under the Uniform Anatomical Gift Act or similar laws.

For further information
consult your physican or
American Medical Association
535 N. Dearborn,
Chicago, IL 60610

APPENDIX 2

AVERAGE FUNERAL CHARGES PER FIRM

DIVISION	HIGHEST	MEDIAN	LOWEST
UNITED STATES	**$2,929**	**$1,116**	**$ 652**
1. NEW ENGLAND	**$1,787**	**$1,099**	**$ 748**
2. MIDDLE ATLANTIC	**$2,929**	**$1,149**	**$ 735**
3. SOUTH ATLANTIC	**$1,407**	**$1,087**	**$ 715**
4. EAST NORTH CENTRAL	**$1,692**	**$1,184**	**$ 729**
5. WEST NORTH CENTRAL	**$1,529**	**$1,097**	**$ 781**
8. EAST SOUTH CENTRAL	**$1,430**	**$1,145**	**$ 922**
7. WEST SOUTH CENTRAL	**$1,557**	**$1,149**	**$ 899**
8. MOUNTAIN	**$1,318**	**$ 975**	**$ 652**
9. PACIFIC	**$1,228**	**$ 920**	**$ 690**

A Statistical Abstract of Funeral Service Facts and Figures of the United States. Vanderlyn R. Pine, ed.,

The average funeral charges for each firm participating in the survey was computed.

This table reflects that firm which has the highest average, that firm which has the median average, and that firm which has the lowest average funeral charges for its total-adult funeral services. These figures do not include charges for interment receptacle, cemetery or crematory expenses, monument or marker, or miscellaneous items such as the honorarium for the clergyman, flowers, additional transportation charges, burial clothing, or newspaper notices

APPENDIX 3

TO MY FAMILY, MY PHYSICIAN, MY LAWYER, MY CLERGYMAN
TO ANY MEDICAL FACILITY IN WHOSE CARE I HAPPEN TO BE
TO ANY INDIVIDUAL WHO MAY BECOME RESPONSIBLE
FOR MY HEALTH, WELFARE OR AFFAIRS

Death is as much a reality as birth, growth, maturity and old age—it is one certainty of life. If the time comes when I, ______________________________ ______________________________, can no longer take part in decisions for my own future, let this statement stand as an expression of my wishes, while I am still of sound mind.

If the situation should arise in which there is no reasonable expectation of my recovery from physical or mental disability, I request that I be allowed to die and not be kept alive by artificial means or "heroic measures." I do not fear death itself as much as the indignities of deterioration, dependence and hopeless pain. I, therefore, ask that medication be mercifully administered to me to alleviate suffering even though this may hasten the moment of death.

This request is made after careful consideration. I hope you who care for me will feel morally bound to follow its mandate. I recognize that this appears to place a heavy responsibility upon you, but it is with the intention of relieving you of such responsibility and of placing it upon myself in accordance with my strong convictions, that this statement is made.

Signed ______________________________

Date ______________________________

Witness ______________________________

Witness ______________________________

Copies of this request have been given to: __________

____

____

____

____

THE PATIENT BILL OF RIGHTS

1. The patient has the right to considerate and respectful care.

2. The patient has the right to obtain from his physician complete current information concerning his diagnosis, treatment, and prognosis in terms the patient can be reasonably expected to understand. When it is not medically advisable to give such information to the patient, the information should be made available to an appropriate person in his behalf. He has the right to know by name the physician responsible for coordinating his care.

3. The patient has the right to receive from his physician information necessary to give informed consent prior to the start of any procedure and/or treatment. Except in emergencies, such information for informed consent should include but not necessarily be limited to the specific procedure and/or treatment, the medically significant risks involved, and the probable duration of incapacitation. Where medically significant alternatives for care or treatment exist, or when the patient requests information concerning medical alternatives, the patient has the right to such information. The patient also has the right to know the name of the person responsible for the procedure and/or treatment.

4. The patient has the right to refuse treatment to the extent permitted by law, and to be informed of the medical consequences of his action.

5. The patient has the right to every consideration

of his privacy concerning his own medical care program. Case discussion, consultation, examination, and treatment are confidential and should be conducted discreetly. Those not directly involved in his care must have the permission of the patient to be present.

6. The patient has the right to expect that all communications and records pertaining to his care should be treated as confidential.

7. The patient has the right to expect that within its capacity a hospital must make reasonable response to the request of a patient for services. The hospital must provide evaluation, service, and/or referral as indicated by the urgency of the case. When medically permissible a patient may be transferred to another facility only after he has received complete information and explanation concerning the needs for and alternatives to such a transfer. The institution to which the patient is transferred must first have accepted the patient for transfer.

8. The patient has the right to obtain information as to any relationship of his hospital to other health care and educational institutions insofar as his care is concerned. The patient has the right to obtain information as to the existence of any professional relationships among individuals, by name, who are treating him.

9. The patient has the right to be advised if the hospital proposed to engage in or perform human experimentation affecting his care or treatment. The patient has the right to refuse to participate in such research projects.

10. The patient has the right to expect reasonable continuity of care. He has the right to know in advance what appointment times and physicians are

available and where. The patient has the right to expect that the hospital will provide a mechanism whereby he is informed by his physician or a delegate of the physician of the patient's continuing health care requirements following discharge.

11. The patient has the right to examine and receive an explanation of his bill regardless of source of payment.

12. The patient has the right to know what hospital rules and regulations apply to his conduct as a patient.

APPENDIX 5

THE EYE BANKS PROGRAM:

(Providing Eyes for the Restoration of Sight to the Blind.)

The Eye Bank for Sight Restoration concentrates most of its services in hospitals of the Greater New York Metropolitan area. This bank is an instrument permitting one to make a priceless gift to those who cannot see. Your eye legacy should not be included in your will since wills are not read until too late for the eyes to be of use. Removal of eyes must be done immediately upon death, therefore, preplanning is a necessity.

Individuals must have permission from next of kin and should notify their physician as to their decision. They should then contact:

The Eye Bank for Sight Restoration
210 East 64th St.
N.Y.C., NY 10021
(212) 838-9200

Removal of eyes does not change the appearance of the body.

THE TEMPORAL BONE BANKS PROGRAM FOR EAR RESEARCH

Individuals with impaired hearing or other ear disorders can help toward the conquest of deafness by the simple procedure of bequeathing their inner ear structure for medical research. These organs are housed in the temporal bones and laboratories receiving and studying them and are called Temporal Bone Banks. These banks are *not* like nerve or eye banks where healthy parts are stored and later transplanted to the living. They are ear research labs where bequeathed inner ear structures are studied together with the donor's medical and hearing records.

(For information write or call:)
The Deafness Research Foundation
366 Madison Avenue
N.Y.C., NY 10017
(212) 682-3737

BEQUEST OF BODIES TO EDUCATION:

The following medical schools are located in the New York area. In order to bequeath a body, it is necessary to secure the appropriate forms direct from the school and file them in advance at the school.

New York University School of Medicine
550 First Avenue
N.Y.C., NY 10016
OR 9-3200

Cornell University Medical School
1300 First Avenue
N.Y.C., NY 10021
TR 9-9000

Columbia University College of
Physicians and Surgeons
630 West 168th Street
N.Y.C., NY 10032
579-3447

New York Medical College
Flower Fifth
Fifth Avenue at 106th Street
N.Y.C., NY 10029
TR 6-5500

Albert Einstein College of Medicine
Eastchester Rd/Morris Park Avenue
Bronx, NY 10461
SY 2-2200

Downtown Medical Center
State University of New York
450 Clarkson Avenue
Brooklyn, NY 11203
UL 6-2020

It is important to contact the medical school before delivering the body, mainly to make certain that there is a need at that particular time. It is also desirable to specify an alternative arrangement in case the medical school for any reason is not ready to receive the body.

Most of the schools listed do not make arrangements or pay for transportation, therefore, the services of a funeral director are needed. All schools listed will provide for the disposal of remains, or arrangements can be made in advance for the funeral director to handle.

NATIONAL TRANSPLANT INFORMATION CENTER

The National Transplant Information Center was established in 1968 by United Health Foundation to serve as a central source of information and assistance to men and women concerned with the growing field of tissue transplantation and utilization.

The center's program is designed to provide objective information and educational materials directly through local agencies to insure that the cooperation and generosity of the public will receive full value and benefit.

For information call or write:
The National Transplant Information Center
150 Fifth Avenue
N.Y.C., NY 10011
928-7483

THE CHURCH AS BENEFICIARY

Is it possible to have a church the beneficiary of an insurance policy?

Yes, it is. The naming of your church as the beneficiary on your life insurance contract is an excellent way to make a substantial gift to your church on your death. It is also possible to reduce your federal estate tax (and state inheritance tax) because the gift will qualify as a charitable deduction, thereby reducing the size of your taxable estate.

In addition, if you named your church as an irrevocable beneficiary (as opposed to a revocable beneficiary, which can be changed), the premiums you paid each year would be deductible from your federal income tax as gifts to charities.

This is but a brief summary of the tax law, and the details can be obtained from your tax advisor.

APPENDIX 7

HOW TO FIND A NURSING HOME

1. Plan ahead. Begin investigating nursing homes immediately if your parent has been hospitalized for a serious illness.

2. Find out exactly what financial benefits your parent is eligible for under both federal and state programs. Your family doctor can be helpful, but all information should be checked with your state department of health.

3. Nonprofit homes usually provide the best care, but they have long waiting lists. If your area has a nonprofit home with a good reputation, visit it to use it as a standard of comparison. You may be able to get your parent on the waiting list.

4. Visit as many homes as possible. Try to visit homes of different types—say, large homes with more than 100 beds, and small homes with 40 or 50 beds.

5. Tell the administrator of each home that you want to visit for at least an hour. If he or she objects, the home has something to hide. You cannot acquire any real feeling for the atmosphere of a home in the five-minute tours many administrators prefer.

6. Insist on seeing every floor of the home. Some homes reserve one floor for visitors, and the floor does not reflect conditions throughout the home. Be sure to see the kitchen, bathrooms, dining rooms, and physical therapy facilities.

7. Ask as detailed questions as possible. The local chapter of the National Council of Senior Citizens

can be helpful. H.E.W. publishes a useful booklet with a consumer checklist. It may be ordered from the Supt. of Documents, U.S. Government Printing Office, Washington, DC 20402. The stock number is 1761-00032, and the price is 40 cents.

8. When you have narrowed your choice down to two or three homes, look up the Medicare and Medicaid inspection reports. Your state health department can tell you where the reports are located. You are legally entitled to see them.